## Early Praise for *Secure Your Node.js Web Application*

Every Node.js team should have Karl's book under their belt. If you are seasoned developer entering Node's ecosystem, this book brings you up to speed with what you can expect from the darker corners of the Internet.

➤ **Lukáš Linhart**
   CTO, Apiary Inc.

The Node.js community has been waiting for a book like this. For all of Node.js's ease, it comes at a cost: security. This book eases that cost and removes the often-overlooked downsides of Node.js development.

➤ **Glen Messenger**
   Chief Information Officer, Ditno

If you want to learn how to secure your Node.js apps, there's no way around Karl Düüna's book. In a clear and concise manner the author shows the ins and outs of making your Node.js app an impenetrable fortress. Not a Node.js user? No problem—much of what's covered in Karl Düüna's book can be used in other environments with little change.

➤ **Brian Schau**
   Developer, Rovsing Applications ApS

A thorough and clear explanation of web app security, from the database to the app server to the client. Highly recommended for developers of node-based apps!

➤ **Loren Sands-Ramshaw**
   CTO, @parlay

# Secure Your Node.js Web Application

## Keep Attackers Out and Users Happy

Karl Düüna

The Pragmatic Bookshelf

Dallas, Texas • Raleigh, North Carolina

Many of the designations used by manufacturers and sellers to distinguish their products are claimed as trademarks. Where those designations appear in this book, and The Pragmatic Programmers, LLC was aware of a trademark claim, the designations have been printed in initial capital letters or in all capitals. The Pragmatic Starter Kit, The Pragmatic Programmer, Pragmatic Programming, Pragmatic Bookshelf, PragProg and the linking *g* device are trademarks of The Pragmatic Programmers, LLC.

Every precaution was taken in the preparation of this book. However, the publisher assumes no responsibility for errors or omissions, or for damages that may result from the use of information (including program listings) contained herein.

Our Pragmatic courses, workshops, and other products can help you and your team create better software and have more fun. For more information, as well as the latest Pragmatic titles, please visit us at *https://pragprog.com*.

The team that produced this book includes:

Fahmida Y. Rashid (editor)
Potomac Indexing, LLC (index)
Linda Recktenwald (copyedit)
Dave Thomas (layout)
Janet Furlow (producer)
Ellie Callahan (support)

For international rights, please contact *rights@pragprog.com*.

Printed in the United States of America.
ISBN-13: 978-1-68050-085-1
Printed on acid-free paper.
Book version: P1.0—January 2016

# Contents

# Acknowledgments

I've been lucky to have had a number of great tech reviewers along the way. I'm grateful to Gábor László Hajba, Woody Lewis, Glen Messenger, Daniel Poynter (@DanielSPoynter), Craig Castelaz, Loren Sands-Ramshaw, Nouran Mhmoud, Brian Schau, John Cater, and Michael Hunter for sharing their time and expertise.

Of course, a book on Node.js wouldn't exist without Node.js' father, Ryan Dahl, and the vibrant open source community of Node.js and IO.js projects. Their work is both instructive and inspirational. We're all lucky to have it.

Most important, I want to thank my family, friends, and coworkers at NodeSWAT for all their questions, early feedback, and encouragement throughout the writing process.

And finally, thanks to you, dear reader. Yes, you, reading this sentence! I hope you enjoy the book!

# Preface

Building an application is a bit like constructing a house—you need to have a decent understanding of what you're building. You have to lay a solid foundation and add all the features such as walls, roof, windows, and doors to make the house. To extend the metaphor further, you also want to install locks on your house to keep the weirdos from coming in and wrecking the place. A lock fixed with a few pieces of bubblegum is not as effective as one attached to the door with stainless steel screws. Similarly, you need to know where you can build strong locks in your application. This book shows you how to create strong locks for your Node.js web application to keep out attackers.

If you've been listening to the news lately, you've heard about data breaches and websites being attacked. You may be one of the millions of people whose information has been stolen from a web application. No one is immune: big retailers, government agencies, and small websites are all targeted. The last thing you want as a developer is for attackers to break into your application because of a mistake in your code. This book identifies the techniques used in most attacks today and shows you how you can block those techniques in your Node.js application.

## Who Should Read This Book?

This book is intended for intermediate Node.js developers, or developers who have built at least one Node.js web application. This isn't an introduction to Node.js but a book teaching Node.js developers how to write secure code.

We quickly review Node.js and JavaScript to make sure everyone understands the core basics, but don't treat that review as a substitute for learning Node.js. If you don't know how to write Node.js or how to work different modules, you'll be lost as you go further into the book.

All the code examples in this book have been tested against Node.js v0.12 and v4.0.

# What's in This Book?

Attackers can break your Node.js application in many ways, and they're always adding more tricks. But they won't bother with new, exotic methods when the tried-and-tested techniques continue to work just as well. This book focuses on the common techniques they use and shows you how to close those avenues of attack within your application.

Chapter 1, *Meet Your Tools*, on page 1 provides a quick overview of Node.js and JavaScript. We review some of the quirks in the language and show how to prevent them from becoming security issues in your application.

Securing your application is not just about writing secure code. Of course we'll learn how to avoid common security mistakes, but in Chapter 2, *Set Up the Environment*, on page 11 and Chapter 3, *Start Connecting*, on page 23 we'll also learn how to set up our environment so that attackers can't just waltz right in.

Then we'll move on to writing secure code.

Chapter 4, *Avoid Code Injections*, on page 43 introduces you to code-injection attacks and how attackers steal from your database.

Chapter 5, *Secure Your Database Interactions*, on page 53 focuses on protecting the database layer so that attackers can't easily grab the data stored inside.

Chapter 6, *Learn to Do Things Concurrently*, on page 73 will take a small detour and focus on how concurrency—one of the bases of computer science—is important to the integrity of your application.

Chapter 7, *Bring Authentication to Your Application*, on page 87, Chapter 8, *Focus on Session Management*, on page 99 and Chapter 9, *Set Up Access Control*, on page 111 will take a look into the weak points of the main security mechanisms most web applications employ—authentication, sessions, and authorization.

Chapter 10, *Defend Against Denial-of-Service Attacks*, on page 125 focuses on denial-of-service attacks, which can knock your application offline so that users can't access it anymore.

Chapter 11, *Fight Cross-Site Scripts*, on page 139 and Chapter 12, *Avoid Request Forgery*, on page 161 focus on two of the most popular client-side attack vectors: cross-site scripting (XSS) and cross-site request forgery (CSRF). We'll look at how those attacks work and how you can protect your clients against them.

Chapter 13, *Protect Your Data*, on page 171 helps you avoid leaking confidential information to the public and set up encryption for your database.

Finally in Chapter 14, *Secure the Existing Codebase*, on page 187 we'll see how we can methodically analyze our existing applications and put to use everything we'll learn in this book.

The chapters in this book mostly build on one another as we go along, and so I invite you to read it from start to finish. While the concepts are connected, the code samples are not, so after the first three chapters you can skip around if you feel comfortable with the topics.

## Online Resources

On the website for this book (https://pragprog.com/titles/kdnodesec) you'll find the following:

- The full source code for all the sample programs used in this book.

- An errata[1] page, listing any mistakes in the current edition.

- A discussion forum where you can communicate directly with me and other Node.js developers. Feel free to ask questions via the forum page.[2]

Are you ready to get started? Let's write some secure code!

---

1. https://pragprog.com/titles/kdnodesec/errata
2. https://forums.pragprog.com/forums/384

*The expectations of life depend upon diligence; the mechanic that would perfect his work must first sharpen his tools.*

> ➤ *Confucius*

# CHAPTER 1

# Meet Your Tools

The foundation of the house is usually regarded as the most important part of the construction, but everything begins with the craftsmanship and tools. An expert can still do good work using unfamiliar tools, but it's hard to do *great* work without being accustomed to the quirks and limitations of them. Knowing all the ins and outs of your tools provides you the means to do a good job while avoiding unnecessary mistakes stemming from ignorance.

Even experienced developers might not know some facets of JavaScript and Node.js. So to help you avoid setting up walls with holes in them, we'll begin our journey by becoming acquainted with the main tools we're going to use. It will be a nice reminder for those who are already familiar with the material and a crash course for those who are not.

## Meet Node.js

First and foremost is Node.js—a platform built on Google's V8 JavaScript engine that allows JavaScript to be run outside the browser. It extends JavaScript with binders for various C libraries, along with modules to manipulate binary data, access system functions, and request handling interpreters. These libraries allow Node.js to access files, execute system commands, and listen/respond to network requests—everything a server needs but was missing in JavaScript.

You should know three important things about programming in Node.js from a security standpoint. First, we'll be using the V8 WebKit engine to run JavaScript. Second, the main program of Node.js will run in a single continuous loop thread. As shown in the illustration, the event loop[1] passes jobs to

---

1.  https://www.youtube.com/watch?v=8aGhZQkoFbQ

a thread pool and handles callbacks. Finally, we'll probably be using a lot of other people's code through *NPM*.

## Node.JS Processing Model

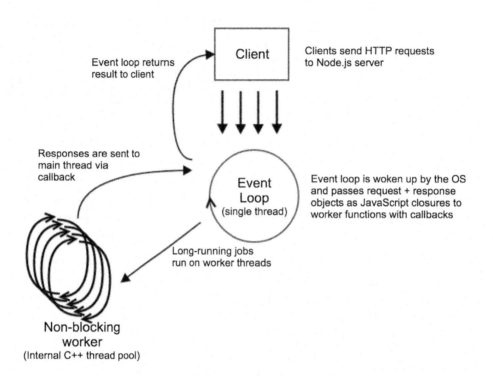

This model is powerful because it allows for great non-blocking I/O to occur in a single thread, which makes the overhead of Node.js very small—no new threads are made. However, the fact there's only one main thread housing the process can be a serious drawback. This leads to some interesting security and reliability issues, which we'll analyze thoroughly in Chapter 4, *Avoid Code Injections*, on page 43 and Chapter 10, *Defend Against Denial-of-Service Attacks*, on page 125.

The other notable thing about Node.js is its ecosystem. A good design decision was made early in Node.js development when NPM was created and then bundled with Node.js. It started as Node Package Manager but has now evolved to be a generic JavaScript package manager. NPM has made programming for Node.js modular—people create small modules designed for a specific task and can then easily share and reuse this code in countless projects.

This sharing and reusing of code creates an environment where coding is productive, since a lot of complicated tasks can simply be solved by installing a module using npm install. But there's also the question of trust—we have to trust that the modules were written by benign individuals, not malicious ones. We have to trust that the modules don't contain errors or backdoors. We address this trust issue more thoroughly later on in *Clean the Modules You Use in Your Code*, on page 197.

Now let's look at JavaScript, the most prominent feature of Node.js, and the main gotchas that you should know about. Taking the time to understand these potential traps will help you be more confident that you're writing secure code.

# Meet JavaScript

ECMAScript, or JavaScript as it's mostly known (I'm going to stick with JavaScript from now on), is one of the most misunderstood programming languages in the world. Because of its rocky history from a simple scripting language to a full-blown development language, it has retained some unusual behaviors and qualities that originally set it apart. Reviewing these is a good practice since even long-time fans may forget about them.

This chapter is not an introduction for beginner JavaScript developers. But if you feel like brushing up on your knowledge of the language itself, I recommend the following resources:

- *Secrets of the JavaScript Ninja [Res09]*
- *JavaScript: The Good Parts [Cro08]*

## Understand That Tools Have Quirks

Jon Erickson explains how hackers look for unintended or overlooked ways to solve a problem in *Hacking: The Art of Exploitation [Eri08]*. Crackers, or attackers, as I'll call them from now on, are just one type of hacker. They look for flaws or unintended behaviors in your code and try to exploit them for their own criminal ends. If you understand the language's quirks, your opponents are less likely to catch you by surprise.

Let's dig in to the security features and weirdness of JavaScript: using *strict mode*, numbers and how automatic conversions affect calculations, comparing values, working with scope, and understanding inheritance. Once you grasp these elements, you can secure your code and avoid making mistakes that make you question your own sanity.

**Always Use 'use strict'**

JavaScript's *strict* mode is the cornerstone of writing secure JavaScript code. *Strict* mode changes both syntax and runtime behavior to be less tolerant of errors and ambiguous constructs. You can enable it by adding use strict to the beginning of the file or function. I recommend that you start all your Java-Script files this way.

Strict mode makes it impossible to accidentally create global variables, since variable definitions without var would automatically throw an error. You also won't be able to use with or assign compiler functions such as eval to other names. And finally, the function scope (this value) isn't boxed to an object and is by default undefined. Let's look at the the following example, where I'll demonstrate those points:

```
'use strict';
a = 1; // this will throw an error because it is executed in strict mode

var x = 17;
with (obj) // !!! syntax error
{
    // If this weren't strict mode, would this be var x, or
    // would it instead be obj.x?  It's impossible in general
    // to say without running the code, so the name can't be
    // optimized.
    x;
}

// This is not an object all the time
// and defaults to undefined
function fun() { return this; }
assert(fun() === undefined);
assert(fun.call(2) === 2);
assert(fun.apply(null) === null);
assert(fun.call(undefined) === undefined);
assert(fun.bind(true)() === true);

var myFunc = eval; // Throws an error
```

To reiterate, you enable strict mode by putting use strict at the beginning of all your files. It takes away some of JavaScript's bad parts and enforces rules that make your code more secure. I recommend reading up on strict mode[2] if this is new to you.

---

2. https://developer.mozilla.org/en-US/docs/Web/JavaScript/Reference/Functions_and_function_scope/Strict_mode

### Beware of Numbers

JavaScript represents all numbers as double floating point numbers. Many people don't realize this, and it frequently results in unexpected errors. For example, (0.1 + 0.2) === 0.3 would return false in JavaScript because the actual value of 0.2 + 0.1 is 0.30000000000000004. Imagine the possible problems that can happen because of this in applications where precise calculations matter, such as shopping carts.

When dealing with calculations, you have to be extra careful not to introduce strings into the mix because of resulting type conversion mix-ups and possibly propagating *Not a Number*s (NaN)s.

Any invalid mathematical operation, such as trying to subtract strings, will produce NaN. In the same way, any mathematical operation involving NaN will result in NaN. In this manner NaNs can propagate and mess up the entire calculation logic unless we put a stop to it with isNaN() checks.

JavaScript's automatic type conversions can also lead to weird results. Automatic conversions can be useful—they're why 60 / "6" returns the correct value. However, if you don't pay attention to the order in which the conversions are made, you'll quickly run into trouble. For example, what is 3 + 5 + "6"?

Did you guess "356"? Well, you'd be wrong. Neither is it 14.

In fact, it's "86".

```
> 3 + 5 + "6"          // converts to (3 + 5) + "6"
  "86"

> (4 + 5 + "3") / 3    // (9 + "3")/3 -> 93/3, not 12/3 = 4
  31
```

To avoid getting caught up in these conversions, use parseInt() or parseFloat() to purge those strings. Remember to include the base argument; otherwise, strings starting with 0x will be parsed as hexadecimal values:

```
> parseInt("0x16")      // hexadecimal
  22
> parseInt("0x16", 10)  // base 10
  0
```

These types of unpredictable results are problematic because they can lead to possible exploits for the attackers. So always check the mathematical operands in your code:

```
> (typeof x === 'number' && !isNaN(x))
// typeof and isNaN are both required, because typeof NaN is 'number'
// whoever did this is probably laughing maniacally at the moment
```

Prepare yourself as this automatic conversion problem isn't limited to only numbers. It can also cause logic problems when trying to compare things.

### Avoid Loose Comparisons

When doing a loose Boolean comparison ==, values like false, 0, the empty string (""), NaN, null, and undefined all become false and all other values become true. Except when they don't. And I am being serious here.

Loose comparisons don't always seem logical, and the results frequently depend on the order of the operands. When evaluated in a Boolean expression, null and undefined both return false; however, in a loose comparison they do not.

```
Boolean(undefined) // false
Boolean(null)      // false

//however
false == undefined // false
false == null      // false
```

Here I illustrate the problem in a security check:

```
var user = {
  name: 'Karl'
};
// forgot to define isAdmin property on my user

function isAdmin() {
  return user && user.isAdmin; // this will return undefined
}

if(isAdmin() == false) { // This will not pass, because false != undefined
  console.log('You should be allowed here, but you are not');
  return;
}
if(!isAdmin()) { // This will pass because undefined is falsy
  console.log('You are allowed here');
  return;
}
```

Here are a few other interesting comparisons you should know:

```
""                ==    "0"          // false
0                 ==    ""           // true
0                 ==    "0"          // true
false             ==    "false"      // false
false             ==    "0"          // true
null              ==    undefined    // true
" \t\r\n"         ==    0            // true
```

Feeling a headache coming on? Don't worry; we've all been there. This is why you should always use strict comparison === to avoid conversion issues with comparisons. Unexpected results lead to logic errors in the application, which again could be exploited by attackers.

### Understand Scopes in JavaScript

Scope is a context within a program where a variable name can be used. JavaScript scope can be somewhat tricky to understand at first, and resulting program flow errors and security issues are common.

By default, variables are global. Omit the var keyword and you declare a global variable. This is the biggest security issue with JavaScript scopes. The previously discussed strict mode will save us from this by disallowing variable declaration without the var keyword, which means no more accidental global variables.

It doesn't save us from accidentally accessing the parent scopes' variables, though. Accidentally overwriting a parent variable is a common mistake and typically results in unexpected system behavior or an application crash:

chp-1-node/scope-iterate.js
```
var i = 0;

function iteratorHandler() {
    i = 10;
}

function iterate() {
    //this iteration will only run once
    for (i = 0; i < 10; i++) { // Since we don't use var here the global i is used

        console.log(i); //outputs 0
        iteratorHandler();
        console.log(i); //outputs 10

    }
}

iterate();
```

Understand scope, and you avoid unwanted changes in the global and parent scopes. No unexpected changes, fewer program flow errors. Google Developer Expert Todd Motto[3] has a great overview if you're interested in learning more about scope.

---

3.   http://toddmotto.com/everything-you-wanted-to-know-about-javascript-scope/

### Inherit from the Prototype

If you're familiar with other common languages, you're probably used to writing class-based inheritance. Unlike those languages, JavaScript doesn't have classes (at least not before ECMAScript 6) but instead relies on *prototypical inheritance*. This complex subject[4] is one of the most misunderstood topics in JavaScript, so let's quickly review it.

In JavaScript, every object has a base object called a *prototype*. If you try to access an object's property and it's not defined, Javascript returns the value from the prototype's property, if it exists. Otherwise, it goes up the hierarchy and asks the prototype's parent if it has the property.

This sounds a lot like classical inheritance, except for the fact that classical inheritance inherits the behavior from the parent class, without state. It inherits the behavior at the moment the object is instantiated. Prototypical inheritance, on the other hand, inherits both the behavior and state from the parent object. It inherits the behavior at the moment the object is called. If the parent object changes at runtime, then the state and behavior of the child object will be affected. It means you can change objects even after they're created, without direct access to the objects themselves. Take a look at this:

chp-1-node/prototype.js
```
'use strict';

function Person() {}                     // define the Person Class

Person.prototype.walk = function(){   // Modify the prototype
    console.log('I am walking!');
};
Person.prototype.sayHello = function(){
    console.log('hello');
};
// now every Person object will be able to invoke these functions

var person = new Person();
person.walk();                          // logs 'I am walking!'

var person2 = new Person();
person2.__proto__.walk = function () {
    console.log('I am walking fast');
};

person2.walk();  // logs 'I am walking fast'
person.walk();   // also logs 'I am walking fast' as we changed the prototype
```

---

4.   http://msdn.microsoft.com/en-us/magazine/ff852808.aspx

Changes to the prototype will affect all objects that have that prototype in their prototype chain. It can be cool but also confusing. In the interest of maintaining your sanity and the integrity of your application, please avoid changing original prototypes. We cover some security implications of this in Chapter 4, *Avoid Code Injections*, on page 43.

## Wrapping Up

You should now have a better overview of your tools. We covered that a Node.js application runs in a single thread and supports events at the base level. We also examined how JavaScript's peculiarities, from mathematical rounding errors to automatic type conversions, can cause hard-to-debug errors. You should now be aware of these issues and know how they can cause problems.

Now that we have a inspected our tools, we can start securing a Node.js application. Let's start with the server and work our way up.

*By failing to prepare, you are preparing to fail.*
> *Benjamin Franklin*

# CHAPTER 2

# Set Up the Environment

You should now have a better understanding of how your tools work and, more importantly, how they can cause problems if not used correctly. In this chapter, we'll start working on the foundation—the server. There are many things to secure before we can write Node.js code.

You're looking at the title and wondering why I'm talking about the server instead of Node.js. Application security is a layered concept—we start from the outside and first secure our environment, network, and other auxiliary systems before we can even start work on the core application, as the following illustration shows.

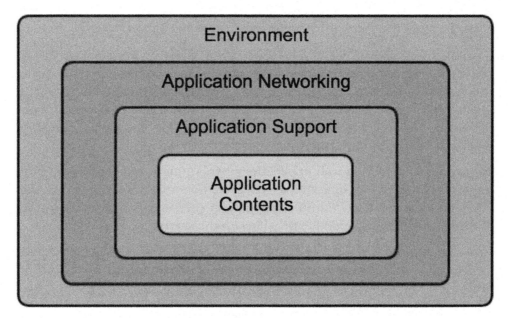

Why? Because if we don't secure the surrounding layers, the inner defenses in our application matter little. We can't just put a password on a computer and say that computer is safe from thieves. We first need to lock the front door, right? That password won't stop a thief from simply taking the computer and walking out the door.

Every application has to live somewhere—a server, a phone, a device—an environment. Before we can secure higher levels of the stack and adopt secure coding practices, we must work our way up.

In this chapter, we'll discuss the *principle of least privilege*, how to properly configure our server, and ways to manage different environments. Yes, this isn't writing code, but good security starts with making sure the server is set up correctly. And while some of these topics might seem basic to you, I've seen time and time again that often it's the basics that get overlooked.

So, let's get started.

## Follow the Principle of Least Privilege

The principle of least privilege (PLP) will help us design better security throughout the application.

In PLP, every abstraction layer in an application—program, user, process—has access only to the information and resources that it needs to complete its task. If the application layer can't access privileged resources, then it can't be abused to give attackers access to those resources. PLP limits damages in case of a breach.

A common example of PLP can be seen in the operating systems; as a user, you have a regular account for working with installed applications. When you want to do something that requires higher privileges, such as installing an application, you see a prompt asking for higher privileges. This kind of manual privilege escalation system makes it harder for attackers to execute malicious programs on victims' machines.

We can also see PLP in web applications, where the server process doesn't have read access outside the web application directory. This prevents attackers who somehow found a loophole in the server configuration from abusing it to read and modify other files on the server.

In reality, true PLP is practically impossible because it's extremely difficult to determine all the resources that a program needs and at what point in time. However, even a moderate implementation of the concept increases application security by a great deal.

From our web application standpoint, we have the following rules:

- The web application should not be run with root privileges. It should instead use a limited account that has access to only the required resources.

- The database account should not be a root account. The account should have limited privileges over the database tables. We touch upon this in Chapter 5, *Secure Your Database Interactions*, on page 53.

- The users of the web application should be given the minimum set of privileges they need.

Following this simple list while developing the application greatly increases the security and fault tolerance because the impact of all errors and vulnerabilities is contained within their specific areas.

## Start with the Basics: Secure the Server

PLP isn't enough if the hardware housing our application is riddled with holes. Attackers are looking for any way in and will target both the production and development servers hosting the application. If we forget to secure the server itself in the rush to code a secure application, all the things we're going to discuss in later chapters will no longer matter.

What good is session management in our application if the server has a weak password? Does it matter if we implement a rock-solid authentication scheme if the server is running old and vulnerable software? No. Remember, we need to lock the front door before we password-protect the computer.

Since this book is about Node.js security and not server security, we'll keep things brief and basic.

The first step is authentication, because it's the most important aspect of server security. Keep the following guidelines in mind for a secure authentication scheme:

- *Do not use the root account all the time.* Using an ordinary account and sudo to elevate permissions when required minimizes the attack vector by limiting the timeframe and execution rights.

- *Do not give the same account to everyone.* It makes it hard to separate permissions of individuals or determine a point of attack later on.

- *Use dedicated machines.* Having the production site running on a machine otherwise used for email or web browsing opens up so many attack vectors that anything that you might save on hardware would be gobbled up by balancing security.

- *Keep access to the production server to a minimum.* There's no reason for someone from accounting to have root access to the production server hosting your web application. Let access be limited to the minimum number of people possible.

- *Change the default password or use key-based authentication.* Most cloud services provision machines with default root accounts and send the passwords by email. Change those!

The application server should be single purposed. Running a pet development app on the same server as a business-critical application is a great idea—if you want to sabotage your production environment. (That was sarcasm.) Don't do it, because you're just offering up a buffet of attack vectors to break into the server and the resident applications.

Set up a proper firewall. Block all network traffic that should not be occurring in the first place. If necessary, you can also set up a reactive firewall to block denial-of-service attacks when they occur.

Another basic step, but an important one, is to make sure all the software installed on the server is up to date. If the history of computers has shown us anything, it's that complex software without bugs is like a miracle—some say they have seen it, some even say that they have made such a program, and the rest of us just shake our head in disbelief. Keep your system up to date to limit exposure time to vulnerabilities as they're found.

In 2014 alone, two serious bugs were found in commonly used networking software and required a software update for almost all servers around the world: Heartbleed[1] and ShellShock.[2] Make sure you're running updated server software to ensure these two and other security bugs don't affect you.

Securing the server operating system, setting up firewalls, and hardening the environment are all broad topics and out of scope for this book. I recommend taking the time to understand network and OS-level security. Here are a few good online tutorials and lists to get you started:

- *Securing and Optimizing Linux: The Ultimate Solution*[3]
- An Introduction to Securing Your Linux VPS[4]
- 20 Linux Server Hardening Security Tips[5]

---

1. http://heartbleed.com/
2. http://www.symantec.com/connect/blogs/shellshock-all-you-need-know-about-bash-bug-vulnerability
3. http://www.tldp.org/LDP/solrhe/Securing-Optimizing-Linux-The-Ultimate-Solution-v2.0.pdf
4. https://www.digitalocean.com/community/tutorials/an-introduction-to-securing-your-linux-vps
5. http://www.cyberciti.biz/tips/linux-security.html

# Avoid Security Configuration Errors

Now that our server won't fall to the first script kiddie that comes along, let's make sure we won't make errors configuring our software stack. Breaches due to misconfiguration are more common than those due to *zero-day vulnerabilities*.

---

**What Is a Zero-Day Vulnerability?**

Some software bugs let attackers remotely execute commands on targeted machines. Although software developers quickly release patches as soon as these issues are found, sometimes attackers find the bugs first. Zero-day vulnerabilities are bugs attackers are using before the software developer has the chance to fix them. Zero days have passed since the patch for that bug, hence the name.

---

There are as many possible areas of misconfiguration as there are different combinations of software installed on your server, making it impossible to cover them all in a single book. Let's focus on common configuration mistakes and how to configure the production and development environments. These examples should give you a good grounding of what you should and shouldn't do in your setup.

## Change Default Users and Passwords

First, you need to keep an eye on default accounts. We all like it when things work right out of the box—little to no setup and everything runs smoothly. While the fact that some frameworks and content management systems (CMSs) ship with default accounts pre-created makes installation convenient, it presents a serious security threat.

What's the threat, you ask? Well, anyone who has either installed the software or read the documentation will know about those accounts. So unless you change them, anyone can use those accounts and walk through all your layers of security. This is a widespread issue, since default accounts can also be found on networking equipment, databases, and cloud server instances, to name a few. Any default accounts in the software and hardware stack *must* be either deactivated or reconfigured.

## Set Up Separate Development and Production Servers

In a proper software development environment, you test and stage code so that you iron out any bugs before production. However, there's a security paradox: you want to keep the development, testing, and staging environments separate and homogenous at the same time. What you end up should be similar to the following diagram.

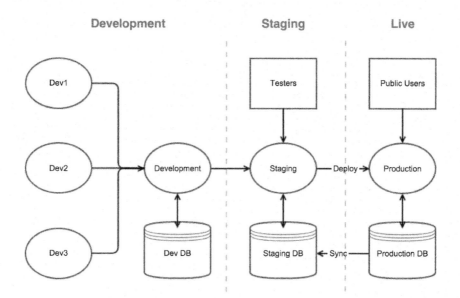

Let's start with the separation. Production and development environments should not be on the same machine. You might wonder why, especially since consolidating would reduce development costs.

The answer is simple: development versions of the application are by definition incomplete and have bugs. Attackers can exploit those issues to access production data or look at the source code to understand how the application works. The development environment should be treated as an internal resource, one that cannot be accessed directly from the web and lives behind an authentication screen to make sure only authorized users can get in.

To reiterate, keep your production code separate from everything else.

You want to make sure the application runs as expected in production, which means the development, testing, and production environments have to have the same software and settings. But it's neither optimal nor safe to configure production exactly the same as other environments, because they fulfill different purposes, as the following illustration shows.

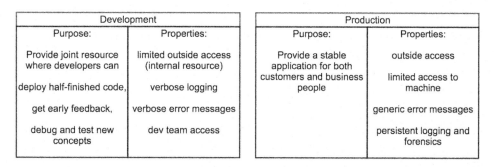

| Development | |
|---|---|
| Purpose: | Properties: |
| Provide joint resource where developers can | limited outside access (internal resource) |
| deploy half-finished code, | verbose logging |
| get early feedback, | verbose error messages |
| debug and test new concepts | dev team access |

| Production | |
|---|---|
| Purpose: | Properties: |
| Provide a stable application for both customers and business people | outside access |
| | limited access to machine |
| | generic error messages |
| | persistent logging and forensics |

Development environment tends to have more relaxed security and verbose logging for debugging. All the developers on the team need to have access to the development environment. In comparison, the whole team typically doesn't work on production servers, so fewer users should be able to log in. As I also discuss in *Decide What Gets Logged*, on page 29, verbose logging in production is not a good idea.

There are a few ways to configure the development and production environments. You can do it manually with the process.NODE_ENV environment variable, use a configuration manager, or look for a built-in solution, such as the environment in the express framework. The manual process isn't recommended because it gets hard to maintain.

I prefer a configuration manager, but it depends on the complexity and size of the application. I like easy-config[6] (which I wrote), but there are dozens available, such as node-config[7] and nconf.[8]

I suggest using environmental variables such as NODE_ENV to differentiate between them externally. This is less error prone than using runtime arguments, and you're less likely to start up an environment with the wrong settings. Even the express framework recognizes NODE_ENV.

To sum up, live, or production, environments should have restricted policies, with fewer people having access and with fewer privileges. All third-party software should have separate accounts used only within the production environment. And finally, live environments should also have less-verbose logging and error handling, which we look at next.

---

6. https://github.com/DeadAlready/node-easy-config

7. https://github.com/lorenwest/node-config

8. https://github.com/flatiron/nconf

**Limit Error Messages in Production**

In the development environment it's useful to have descriptive error messages and the stack trace printed out for easy debugging. However, they shouldn't be shown in the production environment because they would provide attackers with extra information about the application structure and could possibly expose some vulnerabilities or attack vectors.

For example, with *SQL injection*, which we'll cover in Chapter 5, *Secure Your Database Interactions*, on page 53, there's a vast difference between regular SQL injection and blind SQL injection. The first shows descriptive error messages that provide attackers with insight into what exactly happened and what they have to do to construct a valid attack:

```
Error: ER_PARSE_ERROR: You have an error in your SQL syntax;
check the manual that corresponds to your MySQL server version
for the right syntax to use near '"karl""' at line 1
at Query.Sequence._packetToError (mysql/lib/protocol/sequences/Sequence.js:48:14)
at Query.ErrorPacket (mysql/lib/protocol/sequences/Query.js:82:18)
at Protocol._parsePacket (mysql/lib/protocol/Protocol.js:271:23)
at Parser.write (mysql/lib/protocol/Parser.js:77:12)
at Protocol.write (mysql/lib/protocol/Protocol.js:39:16)
...
```

Blind SQL is much more difficult for attackers since error messages provide no information about what went wrong. That's what we want to see more of. Or in this case less of.

In the express framework, the default error handler watches for NODE_ENV to determine if the detailed stack trace information gets shown. If you set NODE_ENV=production, then all you see is the message, Internal Server Error.

As it should be. As long as you're tight lipped in your production environment, then you can feel good—you're doing things the way they should be done.

**Locking the Environment**

We've been talking for a while about how the production and development environments should be on separate machines and have different configuration settings. But at the same time we also need the environments to be homogeneous.

Before you start roll your eyes and say, "What!" let me explain. I am talking about the software stack. In a perfect world, the servers are clones in terms of operating system, packages installed, and configuration settings.

The recommended setup for Node.js projects places used modules in a package.json file, to look something like the following:

```
{
    "name": "security-misconfiguration",
    "version": "0.0.1",
    "main": "environment.js",
    "dependencies": {
        "connect-redis": "*",
        "easy-session": "*"
    }
}
```

(This example package.json is useless; it was severely gutted to shorten the examples that follow.)

package.json lets you use the npm install command to install all the dependencies. Since we marked each dependency with *, the latest available versions from the repository will be installed. This sounds like a good idea, except now we don't know whether any of the packages have been updated since they were installed in the development environment. The production environment may wind up with newer versions installed than the ones in development.

We talked about having updated software earlier, so having newer versions is better, right? While that's true to some extent, if you haven't tested your application against the newer version of software, then you don't know about potential problems. Maybe the new version of the software causes your application to break or introduces some weird inconsistencies. If you don't know that your software works exactly the same way in production as it does in development, that's not a good thing.

So we should change the package.json to tie down the versions:

```
{
    "name": "security-misconfiguration",
    "version": "0.0.1",
    "main": "environment.js",
    "dependencies": {
        "connect-redis": "~1.4.6",
        "easy-session": "0.0.2"
    }
}
```

This defines more precisely the versions of the packages you want to use. The first is added as an approximate version and the last as a specific version of the package. To make it easier to add approximate versions during development, use the --save flag:

```
npm install express --save
```

This will install the express module and add "express": "~3.4.8" under "dependencies".

This seems to solve the problem, except for the fact that required dependencies frequently have subdependencies. So it didn't really fix the issue, did it? The following example lists the dependencies for connect-redis:

```
"dependencies": {
  "redis": "0.9.x",
  "debug": "*"
},
"devDependencies": {
  "connect": "*"
}
```

This might make it look like the node_modules folder should be included within the repository itself. However, since Node.js supports modules written in C and C++ as well, some of them might need compiling and compiled modules tend to break when moved around. To mitigate, we can use shrinkwrap[9] to lock up the whole dependency tree.

For example, let's look at our original project to install two dependencies. Run the following to create the npm-shrinkwrap.json:

```
npm shrinkwrap
```

```
{
  "name": "security-misconfiguration",
  "version": "0.0.1",
  "dependencies": {
    "connect-redis": {
      "version": "1.4.6",
      "from": "connect-redis@*",
      "dependencies": {
        "redis": {
          "version": "0.9.2",
          "from": "redis@0.9.x"
        },
        "debug": {
          "version": "0.7.4",
          "from": "debug@*"
        }
      }
    },
    "easy-session": {
      "version": "0.0.2",
      "from": "easy-session@*"
    }
  }
}
```

---

9.    https://www.npmjs.org/doc/cli/npm-shrinkwrap.html

Now we can see all dependencies listed in the tree. When we run npm install and the npm-shrinkwrap.json file is in the directory next to package.json, then shrinkwrap installs the same versions we used originally. This keeps the environments homogeneous. I won't go into more detail here, but I recommend looking up more information about the versioning and contents of package.json.[10]

## Wrapping Up

Proper server configuration is critical for any secure web application because you're building the base of the application. In this chapter, we looked briefly at securing the web server, password security, and separating development and production environments. The last thing you want is poor setup or a bug in development to compromise production.

We continue our focus on layered security by moving up another step. This time we'll secure the network layer, which defines how we communicate with the world. Let's move on.

---

10. https://www.npmjs.org/doc/files/package.json.html#dependencies

*Humankind has not woven the web of life. We are but one thread*
*within it. Whatever we do to the web, we do to ourselves. All things*
*are bound together. All things connect.*

➤ *Chief Seattle*

# CHAPTER 3

# Start Connecting

In the last chapter you learned how to secure the first layer of defense—the environment. With that out of the way, we can now focus on the next two layers of defense—networking and application support—shown in the following illustration.

It doesn't matter how carefully you avoid security errors inside your application if you aren't careful about how the application communicates with users and other network components. In this chapter you'll learn how to set up network defenses, track what's happening, and make sure the server doesn't kick the bucket for any old request.

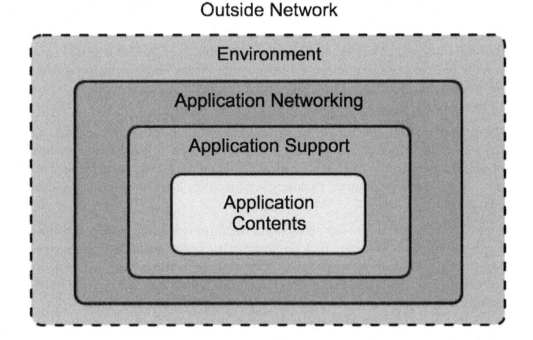

First, we'll see how to set up traffic encryption with Node.js to prevent eavesdropping. We'll then set up a support system for the application to provide diagnostics and robustness for its operational life.

## Set Up Secure Networking for Node.js Applications

Compared to the widely used LAMP (Linux Apache MySQL PHP) or LEMP (Linux Nginx MySQL PHP) stacks, Node.js acts as both the interpreted language (PHP) and the web server (Apache/Nginx); see the following graphic. Node.js handles the communications within the application as well as with outside components.

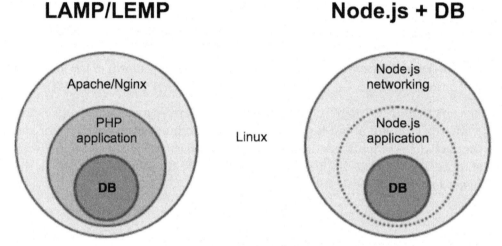

We have full control over network setup and traffic from our Node.js code and don't have to worry about another layer outside the codebase doing something we don't know about, such as serving an index or allowing someone to access a file stored in one of the internal directories.

The lack of outside default configuration is at once both good and bad. It's good because our server does only what we say it can do, similar to how whitelisting works. It's bad because most developers don't know all the caveats of every request type, making their implementations likely to contain common mistakes.

Luckily Node.js has a vibrant ecosystem, with thousands of modules to solve common problems. We get to pick and choose the ones we need for our current application. So while we're not forced to write everything from scratch, we still need to understand how the modules work. Otherwise, we're back to the problem where we don't know what's happening with our application.

Although there are benefits to having Node.js handle all the network configuration, I still recommend using Nginx for static file serving. One reason is that Node.js is a single-threaded process, as we discussed previously. Every second or millisecond the application wastes reading files from disk and sending them to the users is time it's not responding to other requests. That's a lot of time lost if the application responds to twenty image requests for one page load.

And the other reason is that, frankly, Nginx is better at it. Nginx excels at caching and serving static files, and you should always try to use the best tools for the job.

From a security standpoint, why should you care about this? Well, availability is one of the three pillars of web application security. Attackers can try to knock your application offline by overwhelming it with requests. If you reduce the load on your Node.js process, your application becomes more resilient to traffic overload.

## Use TLS and SSL to Secure Your Connections

How would you like it if someone could observe every move you made online, not to mention your login credentials to every site and your credit card information? You probably wouldn't be thrilled (maybe you would, no judgment here), and trust me, neither would your users. You can stop attackers from listening in by encrypting network traffic between your application and the user using *Transport Layer Security* (TLS) or its predecessor *Secure Sockets Layer* (SSL), which are more commonly known as HTTPS.

We won't go into a lot of detail about TLS and SSL here, but I recommend reading up on various attack methods against TLS and SSL.[1] For our purposes, we'll just set up an HTTPS server and assume the rest is taken care of.

To set up an HTTPS server in Node.js, we just need valid SSL certificates generated by a certificate authority (CA). Many developers use self-signed certificates during development, but these certificates throw red flags in browsers and don't protect you from eavesdroppers. Self-signed certificates are okay for development purposes but should never be used in production environments.

---

1. http://en.wikipedia.org/wiki/Transport_Layer_Security

There are several ways to generate a self-signed certificate, including online generators like the one at cert-depot,[2] and plenty of documentation[3] available for your reference. For the following examples, we'll use self-signed certificates since they're easier to obtain, but make sure you apply for CA-generated certificates to use in production. The setup process is the same, so what you learn here will still apply to your production certificates.

**Do Not Use Self-Signed Certs in Production!**

Self-signed certificates aren't secure enough to use in production. Without a trusted CA-signed certificate, you're protected against the most basic attacks and not much else. The security levels vary depending on the type of certificate you buy, so consider your application requirements during the selection process. There are several sources for free certificates, including startssl.com.[4]

With a certificate in hand, you can use the following example to set up an HTTPS server using Node.js:

chp-3-networking/https-plain.js

```
'use strict';

var fs = require('fs');
var https = require('https');

var options = {
    key: fs.readFileSync(__dirname + '/certs/key.pem'),
    cert: fs.readFileSync(__dirname + '/certs/cert.pem')
};

https.createServer(options, function (req, res) {
    res.writeHead(200);
    res.end("hello world\n");
}).listen(8000);
```

It's just as simple using the express framework, as this example shows:

chp-3-networking/https-express.js

```
'use strict';

var fs = require('fs');
var https = require('https');
var express = require('express');

var app = express();
```

---

2. http://www.cert-depot.com/
3. http://www.akadia.com/services/ssh_test_certificate.html
4. https://startssl.com

```
app.get('/', function (req, res, next) {
    res.send('hello world');
});

var options = {
    key: fs.readFileSync(__dirname + '/certs/key.pem'),
    cert: fs.readFileSync(__dirname + '/certs/cert.pem')
};

https.createServer(options, app).listen(8000);
```

And it really is that simple to configure an HTTPS server in Node.js. As you can see, getting the certificates is the biggest hassle in this whole process.

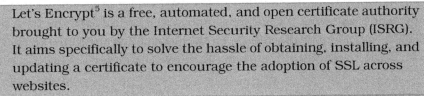

**Let's Encrypt!**

Let's Encrypt[5] is a free, automated, and open certificate authority brought to you by the Internet Security Research Group (ISRG). It aims specifically to solve the hassle of obtaining, installing, and updating a certificate to encourage the adoption of SSL across websites.

Just remember, though, that Node.js does not automatically redirect from HTTP to HTTPS. So be sure to set up a simple HTTP request handler for redirection:

chp-3-networking/http-redirect.js
```
http.createServer(function (req, res) {
    res.writeHead(301, {
        Location: 'https://' + req.headers.host + req.url
    });
    res.end();
}).listen(80);
```

Or use the express framework:

chp-3-networking/http-express-redirect.js
```
var httpApp = express();
httpApp.get('*', function (req, res){
    res.redirect('https://' + req.headers.host + req.url);
});
httpApp.listen(80);
```

Although in this section we looked at how to set up an HTTPS site using Node.js, I must point out that you should use Nginx or other servers in front of your Node.js application to handle the SSL connection. Setting up an SSL connection is expensive, and as Node.js is single threaded, it would suffer in

---

5.   https://letsencrypt.org/

performance when having to deal with many SSL handshakes. Also, dedicated server software is much better at creating and handling SSL connections, with support for newer advanced HTTP features such as HTTP2.

## Add HSTS to the Connection

Although we've now set up our HTTPS connection, it doesn't mean our work is done, since there are attacks designed to break SSL like SSL-stripping attack methods that trick browsers into downgrading an HTTPS connection to HTTP on the initial request. This allows the attacker to eavesdrop the protected traffic. To protect our connection we should set up HTTP Strict Transport Security, or HSTS.

The mechanism of HSTS is to send a Strict-Transport-Security header to the client specifying when the SSL policy will expire. The browser will then default to HTTPS when communicating with the application until this header expires. The following graphic illustrates the difference.

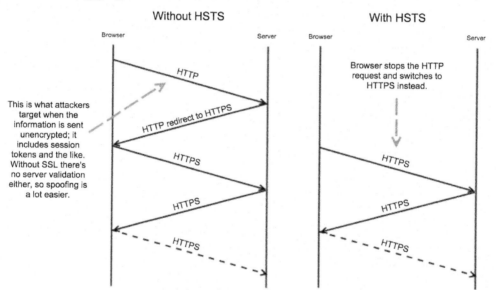

Let's set this header using some simple express framework middleware:

```
app.use(function (req, res, next) {
    var aYear = 60 * 60 * 24 * 365;
    // Set the Strict Transport Security header for a year
    // Also include subdomains
    res.set('Strict-Transport-Security',
      'max-age=' + aYear + ';includeSubdomains');

    next();
});
```

The header is respected by the browser only if it's sent over an HTTPS connection and there are no errors with the certificate. Yet another reason you need a proper certificate!

If you are using Nginx or another proxy in front of your Node.js application as recommended, then you should set protection headers in the proxy configuration to reduce distribution of this knowledge all over the application.

Once the header is received, the browser will start defaulting to HTTPS on your site. The header can be updated on the fly, so you can keep the policy active as long as necessary.

Unfortunately, HSTS doesn't protect the first request ever made by the user to the application. Some browsers work with this limitation by referencing a predefined list of sites using HSTS. Since the list isn't exhaustive, it protects only a limited number of sites. Even with the limitation, setting the header on the first request makes sense because it drastically narrows the possible attack window.

We won't go into more detail here, but Mozilla has a nice page with more information about the HTTP Strict Transport Security header.[6]

## Decide What Gets Logged

We've now set up a secure connection between the application and the users, but we're still missing some important parts of our application's support mechanisms.

Imagine that your company has an office in another country, and things there are very active, with people coming and going at all hours. You know this because you have cameras capturing information about what's happening in that office. Logging is to your application what cameras are to that office. Without logging, you'd have no idea what's happening with your application.

Other web servers do a basic amount of logging by default, but as I discussed before, Node.js does no hand-holding. You have to do this by yourself.

It's a common misconception that logging is useful only when crashes occur (completely false, as we both know). Another misconception is that logging is not related to security. In fact, logging is important for security, because it provides input for both prevention and forensics.

Let's first look at prevention. Logging helps us debug code, detect anomalies in the program workflow, and detect attacks. Inserting proper log lines will

---

6.    https://developer.mozilla.org/en-US/docs/Security/HTTP_Strict_Transport_Security

allow us to learn when the program isn't working as expected. These unexpected behaviors are exactly what attackers exploit to attack the system. So by logging, hopefully we'll be able to find and fix bugs and logic errors in our code before any attacker finds them. Learning about these anomalies by examining log lines is much cheaper than combing the application code after a breach to learn how it could have happened.

Logging also helps you stop an attack during its occurrence. You might be wondering how. Let me demonstrate.

Say our usual log line looks like this:

```
GET / 200 11 - 4 ms
```

Now we get a group of logs like these:

```
GET /'`([{^~' 404 - - 1 ms
GET /aND 8=8' 404 - - 0 ms
GET /' aND '8'='8' 404 - - 1 ms
GET //**/aND/**/8=8' 404 - - 1 ms
GET /%' aND '8%'='8' 404 - - 0 ms
```

We can deduce from these requests that the user is looking for SQL injection points and can act appropriately—by blocking the IP or collecting more information about the attacker for further analysis.

Logging also provides input for forensics. With logging, we can determine the extent of the breach and track down information about the perpetrators. It is likely that at some point attackers will get past our defenses. When they do, we'll need logs to understand how they succeeded, what they did, and where they originated from. Without logging, we'd be effectively blind and have nothing to go on.

Logging is something we simply *must* do when writing a secure web application. Let's look at how we can do it easily.

The express v3 framework exposed a simple logger middleware from connect, the lower-level node module express is built upon. You could enable it with just one line:

chp-3-networking/morgan-simple.js
```
app.use(express.logger());
```

As of express v4, this has been moved to a separate module called morgan and can now be used like so:

```
// Require the morgan logger
var morgan = require('morgan');
app.use(morgan('combined'));
```

This will provide logs in the following format:

```
':remote-addr - :remote-user [:date[clf]] ":method :url HTTP/
:http-version" :status :res[content-length] ":referrer" ":user-agent"'

//example
127.0.0.1 - - [23/Nov/2014:14:34:21 +0000] "GET / HTTP/1.1" 200 13 "-"
"Mozilla/5.0 (Macintosh; Intel Mac OS X 10_10_1)
AppleWebKit/537.36 (KHTML, like Gecko) Chrome/39.0.2171.62 Safari/537.36"
```

You may need a custom solution because you need to log data that isn't supported, or you're not using connect or express. In that case, keep in mind that you should, at the bare minimum, log the time, the user's remote IP address, the requested path, the type of the request (such as GET or POST), and the response code to see how the request was handled. It also helps to log important internal information such as detailed error messages and application procedures. You want to know about database alerts (such as database errors and fatal errors) and important application procedures (such as withdrawal transactions in a financial application).

Put your logger high up the stack so that all requests pass through it. For express it means putting the morgan middleware before other middleware. I recommend looking up and becoming familiar with the morgan logger middleware[7] and the various configuration methods.

You might be thinking now that logging is simple—"I'll just log everything."

I'll just say *don't*. Logging everything isn't as good in practice as it might sound in your head. In this section I'll provide a few guidelines for what not to do.

First of all, don't log too much. Different environments and applications can and usually should require different logging levels. In development you want to see as much of the request's movement as possible in order to trace various problems and/or better understand the internal flow of the application.

However, this information is cumbersome in production because production logs must be persistent. Assuming that the application has proper logging set up, then with development settings the log files would probably grow rapidly.

This would result in information overload—although logs can be searched and consolidated using various tools, you'd still have issues with storage and management if the application usage is high enough.

---

7.  http://www.senchalabs.org/connect/logger.html

Second, store your logs securely. I recommend that the production logs be consolidated to separate machines and if the application type demands it, timestamped. By *timestamping* I mean they should be signed cryptographically so that their time and validity can be checked afterward. This is to prevent log tampering.

And finally, don't log sensitive information. You need to be aware of what you're logging. Avoid logging sensitive information like passwords and credit card/Social Security numbers and so on. If your logs are compromised, they will provide a wealth of information to the attacker.

Also, if you plan to add session-based grouping to logs by logging a session-specific token every time, you must *not* log the sessionID itself as the token. Instead, generate a random value every time a session is created, or hash the sessionID and use that value (the latter should be saved to the session because it's computationally expensive to hash on every request). The last thing you want, if your application gets compromised, is for the logs to be a ready source of sessionIDs and other sensitive information for the attackers.

## Don't Forget About Proper Error Handling

Now that your server is talking to the world and you can see what's going on there, we have another important topic to discuss—errors.

Due to the single-threaded nature of Node.js and the lack of default configuration, a single error could bring the entire application crashing down, something we definitely don't want.

Error handling has been left in the hands of the programmers, and because of the nature of Node.js, it's somewhat complicated to implement correctly.

Let's investigate the various ways to address error handling in Node.js. There are several layers of implementation, and the best one to use would depend on the scale and nature of the application.

### Keep the Process Alive

First, we want to prevent the Node process from exiting unexpectedly. If that happens, all of our open requests will be terminated, even after restarting the process. That results in a bad user experience and introduces possible integrity errors. The process could crash while another person is withdrawing money, for example. That would be hard to recover, and what happened to the money? We must try to avoid the situation altogether.

To achieve this we have to catch all errors that are thrown or emitted. This means you have to wrap fragile parts, where there's a possibility of an error being thrown, in try{}catch(e){} statements.

It also means that all EventEmitters must have an error event listener, because in Node.js error events are special. If an error event is emitted and there are no listeners, then the default action is to print the error and exit the process.

Now this might sound cumbersome, but doing those things will make the application much more stable. And it will also make you analyze possible erroneous parts of the code for what could go wrong—leading to a better understanding of your code.

Also, newer versions of some frameworks (express, for example) already wrap all the route handlers in try{}catch(e){} statements and upon an error direct the output to the specified error handler. This makes it much more convenient for the user and less likely for the whole process to die.

## Try/Catch Asynchronous

While "try/catch" is a good way to execute possible erroneous parts of code without risking a thrown error killing the whole process, you *can't* use "try/catch" with asynchronous code. The following code won't work:

```
function asyncFn(cb) {
    setTimeout(function() {
        throw new Error('I am free');
        cb();
    }, 1000);
}
try {
    asyncFn(function () { //this throws on a timeout
        console.log('I finished');
    });
} catch(e) {
    //this will never fire
    console.error(e);
}
```

The "try/catch" part works only for the initial synchronous part of the try block with the function call (setup of the timeout). When the time comes and the error is thrown, the scope of the error is outside the try statement because it has been executed and is forgotten already.

Stick with the convention of returning errors as the first argument of the callback and don't just throw them.

We might also use the generic process.on('uncaughtException') handler. This will catch all errors that have been thrown or emitted and that haven't been caught somewhere. So in theory you could do something like the following:

```
process.on('uncaughtException', function (err) {
    console.error(err); // just log the error
});
```

However, relying only on catching all errors, especially with the uncaughtException handler, is a *bad idea*. Even the Node.js documentation is clear on this point—because of how JavaScript handles throw(), there's almost never any way to safely pick up where you left off without leaking references or causing other problems. So don't do it.

Everything that throws an error is a threat to the overall stability of the process. Catching those errors (especially with the uncaughtException handler) is bound to corrupt the process eventually. The most common problem that arises is memory leaks that accumulate and finally terminate the process.

This method will delay the crash, but depending on the errors thrown, the process will probably still crash given enough time. Better than before, but there's definitely room for improvement.

## Using Domains in Error Handling

No matter how hard we try, errors will probably still slip through our net of try{}catch(e){} and error handlers and land in the process.on('uncaughtException') that we set up just in case. But the uncaughtException handler gets the error without any other information—we won't know where or why it was thrown. This is where domains come in.

---

**Future of Domains Unclear**

As of Node.js v4.0, the Domains API has been marked as deprecated. It means that the API is likely to change in future releases and should not be depended on for long-term solutions. But when dealing with applications that have a locked version of Node.js, it's still a great tool to use.

---

Domains were added to Node as of v0.8. They provide a way to handle multiple different I/O operations as a single group. If any of the event emitters or callbacks registered to a domain throw an error or emit an error event, then the domain object will be notified. This lets us keep the context of the error, unlike the process.on('uncaughtException'), and handle it better by contextualizing our errors.

Let's see how this works in practice:

```
chp-3-networking/domains.js
'use strict';

var http = require('http');
var domain = require('domain');

http.createServer(function(req, res) {
    var d = domain.create();
    d.on('error', function(err) {
        console.error(err); // log the error
        // Can also do some logging about the request here

        // Respond to the request with an error message
        res.writeHead(500, {'Content-Type': 'text/plain'});
        res.end('Something bad happened!');
    });

    // Because req and res were created before this domain existed,
    // we need to explicitly add them.
    // See the explanation of implicit vs explicit binding below.
    d.add(req);
    d.add(res);

    // Now run the handler function in the domain.
    d.run(function() {
        handleRequest(req, res);
    });
}).listen(3000);

function handleRequest(req, res) {
    switch(req.url) {
        case '/error':
            throw new Error('whoops');
            break;
        default:
            res.end('ok');
            break;
    }
}
```

Here we see that every request is creating its own domain. This allows us to catch the error much like process.on('uncaughtException'), but we also get to keep the context of the request, so we can respond with an error message.

It's a large improvement over simply using process.on('uncaughtException'), because we can do better logging to understand why the error was thrown and also respond to the original request with a polite error. But it still has the undesired side effect of memory leaks and fragile execution states.

## Fork the Process, Catch Errors

You should now understand that once an unexpected error is thrown, the process is on its way to the junkyard. We will need to minimize the impact. The best way is to have more than one process, or forking.

There are two main benefits to forking: it enables the application to make better use of system resources, and it supports *encapsulation* with a graceful restart of failed processes. From a security standpoint, we're most interested in encapsulation.

The goal is to create the master process that would fork itself into multiple processes. When one of the child processes encounters an error, all the traffic to that process is stopped and a new fork is created, as the following graphic shows. The old fork is allowed to finish handling the requests in its queue before being terminated. It keeps reforking new processes, but the leaked references don't accumulate. If service is interrupted, forking makes sure only a small number of users are affected.

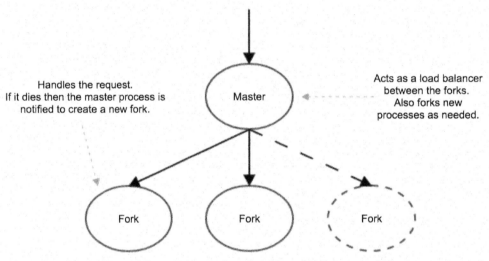

This can be achieved by using either built-in Node.js modules or external solutions. For our examples, we'll look at the built-in cluster module.[8]

We'll start by first creating a process that's forked into multiples. This is a basic example of a web server that's forked as many times as there are CPUs:

chp-3-networking/cluster-simple.js
```
'use strict';

var cluster = require('cluster');
```

8.    http://nodejs.org/api/cluster.html

```
var http = require('http');
// Ask the number of CPU-s for optimal forking (one fork per CPU)
var numCPUs = require('os').cpus().length;

if (cluster.isMaster) {
    // Fork workers.
    for (var i = 0; i < numCPUs; i++) {
        cluster.fork();
    }

    // Log when a worker exits
    cluster.on('exit', function(worker, code, signal) {
        console.log('worker ' + worker.process.pid + ' died');
    });
} else {
    // Workers can share any TCP connection
    // In this case its a HTTP server
    http.createServer(function(req, res) {
        res.writeHead(200);
        res.end("hello world\n");
    }).listen(3000);
}
```

But this example does nothing except log when a worker dies. If we add a fork restart and a generic error handler for the fork to gracefully terminate the process, we'll improve security. The next code example is long, because it also introduces domains to keep the ability to respond to your failed request:

chp-3-networking/cluster-domains.js
```
'use strict';

var cluster = require('cluster');
// Ask the number of CPU-s for optimal forking (one fork per CPU)
var numCPUs = require('os').cpus().length;
var PORT = +process.env.PORT || 3000;

if (cluster.isMaster) {
    // In real life, you'd probably not put the master and worker in the same file.
    //
    // You can also of course get a bit fancier about logging, and
    // implement whatever custom logic you need to prevent DoS
    // attacks and other bad behavior.
    //
    // See the options in the cluster documentation.
    //
    // The important thing is that the master does very little,
    // increasing our resilience to unexpected errors.

    // Fork workers.
    for (var i = 0; i < numCPUs; i++) {
```

```
        cluster.fork();
    }

    cluster.on('disconnect', function(worker) {
        console.error('disconnect!');
        cluster.fork();
    });

} else {
    // the worker
    //
    // This is where we put our bugs!

    var domain = require('domain');

    // See the cluster documentation for more details about using
    // worker processes to serve requests.  How it works, caveats, etc.

    var server = require('http').createServer(function(req, res) {
        var d = domain.create();
        d.on('error', function(er) {
            console.error('error', er.stack);

            // Note: we're in dangerous territory!
            // By definition, something unexpected occurred,
            // which we probably didn't want.
            // Anything can happen now!  Be very careful!

            try {
                // make sure we close down within 30 seconds
                var killtimer = setTimeout(function() {
                    process.exit(1);
                }, 30000);
                // But don't keep the process open just for that!
                killtimer.unref();

                // stop taking new requests.
                server.close();

                // Let the master know we're dead.  This will trigger a
                // 'disconnect' in the cluster master, and then it will fork
                // a new worker.
                cluster.worker.disconnect();

                // try to send an error to the request that triggered the problem
                res.statusCode = 500;
                res.setHeader('content-type', 'text/plain');
                res.end('Oops, there was a problem!\n');
            } catch (er2) {
                // oh well, not much we can do at this point.
```

```
                    console.error('Error sending 500!', er2.stack);
                }
            });

            // Because req and res were created before this domain existed,
            // we need to explicitly add them.
            d.add(req);
            d.add(res);

            // Now run the handler function in the domain.
            d.run(function() {
                handleRequest(req, res);
            });
        });
        server.listen(PORT);
    }


    // This part isn't important.  Just an example routing thing.
    // You'd put your fancy application logic here.
    function handleRequest(req, res) {
        switch(req.url) {
            case '/error':
                // We do some async stuff, and then...
                setTimeout(function() {
                    // Whoops!
                    flerb.bark();
                });
                break;
            default:
                res.end('ok');
        }
    }
```

We've done everything we set out to do: fork, catch errors, and gracefully refork. However, keeping the clustering code in the same file as the application is cumbersome and ugly, something we don't want to do with real-life applications. So let's use a separate file, as shown in this example:

```
chp-3-networking/cluster-separate-file.js
'use strict';

var cluster = require('cluster');
// Ask the number of CPU-s for optimal forking (one fork per CPU)
var numCPUs = require('os').cpus().length;

cluster.setupMaster({
    exec : __dirname + '/index.js' // Points to the index file you want to fork
});

// Fork workers.
```

```
for (var i = 0; i < numCPUs; i++) {
    cluster.fork();
}

cluster.on('disconnect', function(worker) {
    console.error('disconnect!'); // This can probably use some work.
    cluster.fork();
});
```

This code should be in master.js with the main server code in index.js, which needs only slight—or no—alternations to be able to fork or gracefully restart processes. We now have a graceful way to handle errors, and our application uses system resources more efficiently. Better performance and improved security—what a win!

Forking the process as many times as there are CPUs can, however, clog the processor. Unfortunately, there's no golden rule to follow when deciding the number of forks you should have. The number is determined by the structure and infrastructure of the application. If you have other vital processes on the machine, such as the database, then some of the resources are already in use, and you need to account for that before you start forking.

After all this, there's always the possibility the process might exit unexpectedly. It could be because some other process consumed all available memory, for example. The process must somehow be restarted, or the website will be unavailable until the administrator has time to restart everything. That's not an ideal situation to be in.

We have lots of different ways to do this depending on the operating system and tools. Under Unix, we can just daemonize our node script. But there are also Node.js modules for this purpose that are operating-system agnostic. Two popular choices are forever,[9] which has been around for a long while, and PM2.[10] While forever is lightweight, PM2 is a feature-rich alternative, with automatic clusterization, load balancing, log aggregation, and other features. It's definitely worth checking out.

## Wrapping Up

Fabulous—in this chapter you learned about various ways you can secure your networking layer and keep your service running despite errors (that others have somehow sneaked into your code). We covered how encryption protects messages so that others can't listen in, how logging helps you

---

9. https://github.com/nodejitsu/forever
10. https://github.com/Unitech/pm2

understand and defend your application, and how to use error handling to prevent application crashes.

Let's now move on to the most popular attack vector out there: code injection. In the next chapter, we'll look at different code injection attacks and how to prevent them.

*To expect the unexpected shows a thoroughly modern intellect.*

➤ *Oscar Wilde*

CHAPTER 4

# Avoid Code Injections

Great job so far—you learned how to use your tools, set up your environment correctly, and fortify your network communications. You're now finally ready to look at your application and learn about the most popular attack vector out there: *code injection.*

Injection is an attack vector where the attacker introduces, or injects, malicious code into the application to trick the program into executing it. Generally, the user sends specific data to the application, which is passed on to the interpreter to execute. If the application doesn't properly validate the data, then any commands embedded inside are executed.

With code injection, the attacker can make the server do something other than what it's supposed to do. That means obtaining sensitive information, disrupting and damaging the service, or even modifying the service itself.

Several subcategories of injection attacks exist, depending on the target execution environment. Because there are so many ways to use injection attacks, the Open Web Application Security Project (OWASP)[1] ranks injection attacks, especially SQL injection, as the number-one attack vector for web applications.

In this chapter you'll learn to avoid creating potential code injection points in your application and server layers. We'll look specifically at protecting the the database layer from injection attacks in the next chapter, Chapter 5, *Secure Your Database Interactions*, on page 53.

---

1. https://www.owasp.org

## Identify Code Injection Bugs in Your Code

First, you need to learn how to recognize a potential code injection vulnerability. In this section, we'll discuss how injection vulnerabilities are introduced into code so that you'll know what you shouldn't do.

Code injections target applications where the functionality is created and interpreted during runtime based on user input. This makes finding possible attack points straightforward. In Node.js there are two interpreter functions to look out for: eval and Function. With these a developer can create a function out of string input and execute it at will.

The easiest way to avoid code injection attacks is to simply not create and evaluate code using user-submitted data. But using dynamically created code can be necessary in some cases and greatly simplify code in others. So instead of just saying "Never use user-submitted data in code construction," let's learn how to deal with it.

Maybe we're writing a service where the user supplies a mathematical formula and the app evaluates it. We could spend time creating a parser for the operands and operations and then interpret this intermediate form. Or we could simply expect a valid entry and evaluate it for JavaScript calculations:

```
chp-4-code-injection/calculator.js
'use strict';

var express = require('express');
var bodyParser = require('body-parser');
var app = express();

app.get('/', function(req, res){
    var form = '' +
        '<form method="POST" action="/calc">' +
        '<input type="text" name="formula" placeholder="formula" />' +
        '<input type="submit" value="Calculate" />' +
        '</form>';
    res.send(form);
});

app.use(bodyParser.urlencoded({extended: false}));

app.post('/calc', function (req, res) {
    var result;
    eval('result = ' + req.body.formula);
    res.send('The result is: ' + result);
});

app.listen(3000);
```

This is a fairly simple example that works great, as long as the user submits valid calculations. A malicious individual could post something other than a mathematical calculation, however, such as 3; process.exit();, which would terminate the application. This would be a simple denial-of-service attack, which you'll learn more about later, but it clearly demonstrates that we've lost control over our application and how much trust we're putting in the user to submit valid data.

The first line of defense for injection attacks, and many other attack vectors, is to *never trust user-submitted data.* Any data coming from the user should be viewed as poisonous, and any data interacting with the input will also become poisonous. You need to worry both about data coming directly from user input and data pulled from the database, if it was originally submitted by the user.

The safest way is to check the input against a whitelist (not a blacklist) to verify that the data is in the expected format. It's better to use whitelists than blacklists because it's usually easier to identify all possible valid inputs than it is to come up with every single invalid one. Let's extend the previous example to check the input to see if it contains anything other than numbers and operands. It's a basic check and doesn't eliminate all invalid inputs, but already the execution is much safer:

chp-4-code-injection/calculator-regex.js

```
app.post('/calc', function (req, res) {
    var formula = req.body.formula;
    // Check if there is anything else besides 0-9 - * + /
    if(formula.match(/[^0-9\-\/\*\+]/)) {
        res.status(400).send('Invalid input');
        return;
    }

    var result;
    eval('result = ' + formula);
    res.send('The result is: ' + result);
});
```

While rejecting input that doesn't conform to a required format is a valid solution, it isn't the most convenient for the user who may want to insert spaces to make the text easier to read. The user probably won't understand why the input was rejected. A more tolerant approach is to clean the input yourself, as shown in the example on the following page.

```
chp-4-code-injection/calculator-regex2.js
app.post('/calc', function (req, res) {
    var formula = req.body.formula || '';

    // Remove everything besides 0-9 - * + /
    var cleanFormula = formula.replace(/[^0-9\-\/\*\+]/g, '');
    if(cleanFormula.length < 1) {
        res.status(400).send('Invalid input');
        return;
    }

    var result;
    // Surround with try-catch in case still invalid formula.
    try {
        eval('result = ' + formula);
    } catch(e) {
        res.status(400).send('Invalid input');
        return;
    }
    // Say what we calculated
    res.send('The result of ' + cleanFormula + ' is: ' + result);
});
```

The code injection attack's success factor depends on the system being targeted as well as the access rights assigned to the process. If the process has root privileges (which I've pointed out previously is a Very Bad Idea), the attacker would be able to take over the whole server and even use it to launch further attacks.

Another interesting method in the attacker's arsenal is called *server poisoning*, where the attacker rewrites the server code as part of an injection attack to change the server's behavior altogether.

Attackers can use server poisoning to steal information, such as modifying the application to send them an email containing the user's password in plain text, or for monetary gains, such as changing how orders are calculated. You could lose money on every transaction and not know why.

Attackers can also rewrite server code in other interpreted languages such as PHP, but the approach is different to that with Node.js. In PHP, the attacker has to change the code file, so you can defend against server poisoning by making sure the code files on your server aren't writable by the server process. Because Node.js treats functions as variables and runs in a single thread, the attacker doesn't need to touch the file system to modify server behavior. This makes server poisoning attacks stealthier and harder to defend against in Node.js applications.

So far we've looked at how code injection attacks can be insiduous and stealthy and how to use input validation to protect the code. Next, we'll look at another type of code injection attack that targets the server.

## Avoid Shell Injection in Your Application

*Shell injection* is a form of injection attack where the target is the underlying operating system. More specifically, the attackers are focusing on the commands executed by the web application in the operating system layer. In Node.js this means commands executed through the child_process module, using exec, execFile, spawn, or fork. These commands can execute scripts on the operating system and can become a possible attack vector for code injection if the commands are incorrectly constructed with user input.

As with interpreter functions, shell commands are useful because they simplify the application logic by pushing certain tasks to external libraries. The two differences are the character set used and the execution environment. The attacker may not have access to runtime variables in a shell injection attack, but there are still plenty of ways to cause serious damage.

You might be thinking "Great. Another group of commands I simply won't use." As before, there are situations where shell commands drastically simplify the development or are required because of parallelism needs, for example, when we write an application that provides IP address information about URLs. We could look for a third-party module or write code to connect to the Domain Name System (DNS) and look up the information. Or we could use a command that comes with practically every operating system, host:

chp-4-code-injection/shell.js
```
'use strict';

var express = require('express');
var bodyParser = require('body-parser');
var exec = require('child_process').exec;
var app = express();

var form = '' +
    '<form method="POST" action="/host">' +
    '<input type="text" name="host" placeholder="host" />' +
    '<input type="submit" value="Get host" />' +
    '</form>';

app.get('/', function(req, res){
    res.send(form);
});
```

```
app.use(bodyParser.urlencoded({extended: false}));

app.post('/host', function (req, res) {
    exec('host ' + req.body.host, function (err, stdout, stderr) {
        if(err || stderr) {
            console.error(err || stderr);
            res.sendStatus(500);
            return;
        }
        res.send(
            '<h3>Lookup for: ' + req.body.host + '</h3>' +
            '<pre>' + stdout + '</pre>' +
            form
        );
    });
});

app.listen(3000);
```

And now a user could simply ask for information on Google.com, for example, and get a nice output, as shown in the figure on page 49.

Again, the problem is trusting the user to send valid input. What if the attacker sends something like google.com | cat /etc/shadow? If you don't validate the user input, the attacker will probably be able to see the contents of the server's /etc/shadow file, containing password information. Not a good result.

The first recommendation is to use execFile instead of exec when possible. The exec command uses the /bin/sh shell interpreter to run the command, which can be targeted by attackers to break out and launch other commands. execFile, however, executes the file directly, giving attackers a much smaller attack surface (limited by the file being executed). On the downside, you will lose some interoperability between environments and the ability to run complex commands with piping, but in turn your code will be more secure.

chp-4-code-injection/shell-fix-execfile.js
```
var execFile = require('child_process').execFile;

app.post('/host', function (req, res) {
    execFile('/usr/bin/host', [req.body.host], function (err, stdout, stderr) {
        // . . .
    });
});
```

Another way to mitigate the attack surface is to whitelist and typecast the user-supplied variables when constructing shell commands. First, let's whitelist our input and allow only certain characters:

# Lookup for: google.com

```
google.com has address 193.229.108.94
google.com has address 193.229.108.98
google.com has address 193.229.108.123
google.com has address 193.229.108.119
google.com has address 193.229.108.99
google.com has address 193.229.108.109
google.com has address 193.229.108.108
google.com has address 193.229.108.104
google.com has address 193.229.108.88
google.com has address 193.229.108.93
google.com has address 193.229.108.113
google.com has address 193.229.108.118
google.com has address 193.229.108.114
google.com has address 193.229.108.84
google.com has address 193.229.108.103
google.com has address 193.229.108.89
google.com has IPv6 address 2a00:1450:4010:c04::8b
google.com mail is handled by 30 alt2.aspmx.l.google.com.
google.com mail is handled by 40 alt3.aspmx.l.google.com.
google.com mail is handled by 50 alt4.aspmx.l.google.com.
google.com mail is handled by 10 aspmx.l.google.com.
google.com mail is handled by 20 alt1.aspmx.l.google.com.
```

| host | Get host |
|------|----------|

chp-4-code-injection/shell-fix-whitelist.js
```
app.post('/host', function (req, res) {
    var host = req.body.host || '';

    // Test for everything besides alphanumeric and . and -
    // Also test for starting . and -
    if(host.match(/^[-\.]|[^a-zA-Z0-9\-\.]/)) {
        res.status(400).send('Invalid input');
        return;
    }

    execFile('/usr/bin/host', [host], function (err, stdout, stderr) {
        // ...
    });
});
```

This fix is effective because it prevents users from creating other commands or manipulating them in unseemly ways. But whitelisting isn't always possible, so instead we can limit *run rights*. We limit the rights the Node.js process has when executing the command by running it as a user with a limited set of rights. We can do this by providing corresponding uid or gid options.

Most Unix systems have a nobody user that we can use to run common services. We can set up our code to run the command as nobody by looking for the UID and setting it in the command options:

```
chp-4-code-injection/shell-fix-uid.js
var opts = {};
app.post('/host', function (req, res) {
    // Add options specifying uid, which we asked from system
    execFile('/usr/bin/host', [req.body.host],
        opts, function (err, stdout, stderr) {
            if(err || stderr) {
                console.error(err || stderr);
                res.sendStatus(500);
                return;
            }
            res.send(
                '<h3>Lookup for: ' + req.body.host + '</h3>' +
                '<pre>' + stdout + '</pre>' +
                form
            );
        });
});
// Look for the nobody user

// NOTE:
// On OSX this can cause an error because the UID of nobody
// is a negative number (-1) represented by overflowing integer
execFile('/usr/bin/id', ['-u', 'nobody'], function (err, stdout, stderr) {
    if(err || stderr) {
        console.error(err || stderr);
        process.exit(1);
    }

    // Set the uid in the options
    opts.uid = +stdout;

    // Start server
    console.log('Nobody is ' + opts.uid);
    console.log('Listening on 3000');
    app.listen(3000);
});
```

Now, an attacker trying to see the /etc/shadow file will see an error because it's a restricted file and the nobody user doesn't have access to it.

For best results, use the combination of all mitigation methods: execFile, limit access rights and possible inputs. As you can see, the defense methods for both shell injection and code injection follow the same principles.

## Wrapping Up

In this chapter we looked at one of the most versatile and popular attack vectors in the enemy's arsenal—code injection. You should now know how to identify possible attack locations and how to properly validate user input. You also learned about minimizing possible damages by limiting access rights of your processes.

In the next chapter, we'll dig deeper into this attack vector and learn how it targets the database and what we can do to keep it safe.

*Real knowledge is to know the extent of one's ignorance.*

➢ *Confucius*

# CHAPTER 5

# Secure Your Database Interactions

In the last chapter we covered how to identify code injection attacks and ways to defend your server and processes. We'll continue by learning about database security and especially about how most injection attacks target it.

The database is the heart of most modern web applications—without it the applications are just empty husks. Books with covers but no pages. Application data stored in the database, especially user information, is a prime target for attackers. They want the passwords and personal information to log into accounts on other sites. They desire financial and credit card information to empty user bank accounts. They may want sensitive—or potentially embarrassing—information that can be used to blackmail users.

Knowledge is power.

Many companies suffered data breaches in 2014, and millions of individuals saw their Social Security numbers, credit card numbers, and passwords stolen. While many of these attacks, especially high-profile ones, used highly sophisticated methods, some used a far simpler *database injection attack.* This is similar to shell injection, except the targeted execution layer is the database. As mentioned in the previous chapter, OWASP (Open Web Application Security Project)[1] considers database injection the top attack vector against web applications.

We want to stop attackers from getting their hands on our users' data. If the attackers succeed, we lose our users' trust, our business won't be successful, and we won't be able to afford that new Tesla we like so much. We can't have that, so let's spend this chapter preventing database injection and related attack vectors.

---

1.　https://www.owasp.org

You can work work through the examples in this chapter with MySQL,[2] PostgreSQL,[3] and MongoDB[4] databases. We'll walk through the data model and table schemas together. Setting up the database and account is out of scope for this book, so you should reference your database documentation to get started.

## Start with the Basics: Set Up the Database

Let's start from the beginning—your application has to successfully connect to the database before you can do anything. Let's make sure you don't fumble the ball even before you cross the line of scrimmage.

Any database that you work with, and it doesn't matter if we're talking about MySQL, Mongo, Redis, or any other database system, should be configured to use authenticated users. Sometimes people don't bother with user accounts and let everyone (including applications) connect to the database without a password. They typically block outside connections, which is a good thing to do. Unfortunately, it's not sufficient, even if the database lives on the same machine.

Yes, blocking outside connections narrows the attack surface significantly. But the attacker can bypass this restriction by gaining access to one of the whitelisted machines or the IP addresses. If I'm running a Redis database server on my machine with default settings enabled—no authentication—then all the attacker has to do is somehow get onto my machine. It doesn't matter if the attacker is using an unprivileged account since there's no barrier to connecting to the database. Voila! Full access to every database and all the data.

Imagine your server as an apartment building, individual apartments as databases, and each room in the apartment as a table in the database. Just because you have a lock on the front door of the building does not mean you don't want locks for each apartment. It would still disturb you very much if someone from the street managed sneak through the front door and then could roam around the building visiting every room and looking at your things. Just because someone has access to the server doesn't mean they should have access to all the data in each database.

It's clear that proper authentication is an important aspect of defense. It will be harder for attackers to pull off a successful attack if the application is

---

2. http://www.mysql.com/
3. http://www.postgresql.org/
4. http://www.mongodb.org/

smart about who it lets in, who it keeps out, and who is allowed to do what. Setting up authentication also lets you follow the principle of least privilege to fine-tune different levels of access for each account. You may want to revisit *Follow the Principle of Least Privilege*, on page 12 for a refresher.

Our theoretical web application has three separate database accounts for users—guest, authenticated, and admin; see the following graphic.

- Guest users can only read articles on the site—so the guest database account needs only read access for the database tables.

- Authenticated users can read and write articles, as well as post comments—meaning the authenticated database account should have read and write access on tables related to articles and comments.

- Admin users can add new users and do other administrative tasks. The admin account on the database has the highest privilege level, with read/write privileges on most, if not all, tables.

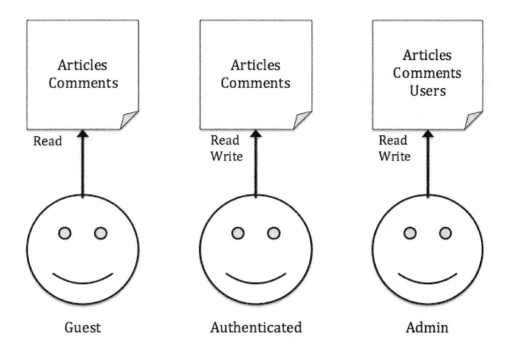

You might wonder why you need to go through the trouble of having separate database accounts if you already have separate user roles. Suppose you have a database injection vulnerability somewhere in the guest section of the application. Attackers who exploit this hole won't be able to cause as much damage because the guest database user has only read privileges on the tables.

Your admin account may not even need all the privileges it currently has. You probably would never drop tables from the web application, for example. Remove that privilege from the admin database account and the attacker won't be able to use code injection to delete data. You'd still have elevated privileges as the admin user when connected directly to the database, which is all you need.

Defining multiple accounts in the database with various levels of privileges is a good thing, but you need to use them. Look at the following code snippet to see an example how you could manage multiple connections to the database:

chp-5-database/mysql-multiple-connections.js
```
// Set up guest connection
var guestConnection = mysql.createConnection({
    host     : 'localhost',
    user     : args.gu,
    database : args.d,
    password : args.gp,

    // Set for testing, do not do unless you have a good reason
    multipleStatements: true
});
guestConnection.connect();

// Set up admin connection
var adminConnection = mysql.createConnection({
    host     : 'localhost',
    user     : args.au,
    database : args.d,
    password : args.ap,

    // Set for testing, do not do unless you have a good reason
    multipleStatements: true
});
adminConnection.connect();

// Middleware for checking the logged in status
app.use(function (req, res, next) {
    // If we have an admin session then attach adminConnection
    if(req.session && req.session.isAdmin) {
        req.db = adminConnection;
    }
    // Otherwise attach guestConnection
    else {
        req.db = guestConnection;
    }
    next();
});
```

You now have a lock on your database, and, more importantly, you should now understand why you need one. The lock will deter people trying to snoop through data they shouldn't be allowed to see, which will keep the clients happy. And that keeps *you* happy.

Let's take a quick look at another important data-separation paradigm that you should know besides simple role-based connection—multi-tenancy.

## Separate Databases for Better Security

Many web applications serve as platforms for multiple clients at the same time. Depending on the application, this will involve storing business data or logic in the database. For example, you may have a CRM system where clients store their own records, connections, and billing information. You need to safely separate the data so that clients can't access each other's data. There are many approaches ranging from totally isolated databases to fully shared ones, but they tend to fall somewhere along the spectrum, as shown here.

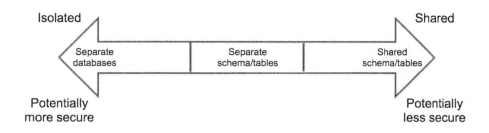

The security of these methods can vary and depend on other development and infrastructure requirements. But let's look at each one in detail.

First up is having separate databases for everyone, as shown in the graphic. This is the most isolated approach. Every client has a separate database for its data and each client can customize the data structure for its own needs. It can be more secure, but it comes with higher infrastructure costs. Databases take up space (an empty MongoDB database takes 32 MB, for example), and there's only so much space available on a server.

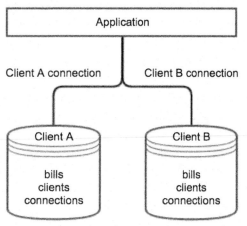

Completely isolating your tenants is a good approach when you have strict security needs and clients who are willing to pay extra for security. You can use this approach with most SQL and NoSQL databases (including MongoDB).

The middle approach is to use the same database but separate the schemas (tables/collections) for each client, as the graphic shows. Each tenant has access to only its own set of tables. Like the isolated approach, each tenant can customize the data structures and keep database connection levels separate from everyone else.

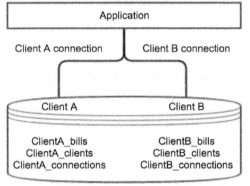

This method makes backups tricky. In the isolated approach, you back up and restore a single tenant's database without affecting anyone else. Here, you have to back up all the tables together, regardless of client. Restoring a single tenant's data is a challenge as you don't want to affect others.

Neither can you fully use this approach in MongoDB because it doesn't have collection-level access control. While there are modules like mongoose-multitenant,[5] you still can't control connection access at the collection level. You'd miss out on most of the security benefits of this approach, and MongoDB has limits on how many collections you can create in a single database as well.

The last approach is the most common—storing all the clients' data in the same database and sharing the database schema. The data is separated by providing a unique tenant identifier for each row. It's the cheapest approach because it has the lowest infrastructure requirements, but it has the highest implementation cost for security. You have to handle security in your code and manage all the data-separation mechanisms yourself.

Most applications start out from a shared model, since businesses generally start thinking about multi-tenancy only after the application has gotten large enough. Or they have to comply with regulatory requirements. There's no best approach, because that depends on your specific needs. I recommend generally starting out with the shared approach and eventually graduating to the isolated approach when you can.

Next, let's look at how to mitigate attacks against data stored in your database (or databases).

---

5.    https://www.npmjs.com/package/mongoose-multitenant

## Identify Database Injection Points in Your Code

We briefly talked about database injection earlier. It's a variation of code injection, but the intended target is the back-end database and not the application server. Let's look at this widely used attack in detail and discuss ways to prevent it.

If an application has code injection issues, it means the application is not correctly validating all input fields on the site. The same thing applies to database injection. Attackers enter a series of database commands into the application's input fields (such as a textbox in a blog's comment form) to trick the application into executing the commands within the database. If the application builds its database queries by concatenating user input with hardcoded strings instead of using a decent ORM (object-relational mapper) and neglects to properly escape input data, then the attacker succeeds.

Let's take a look at what a database injection flaw looks like. Make sure you understand what's happening here, because we'll revisit this again in later chapters.

For the following examples you'll need a MySQL database. For all database examples, we'll use the minimist[6] module to parse command-line arguments—which we'll use to supply the database connection information.

```
chp-5-database/mysql-exploitable.js
var mysql = require('mysql');
var express = require('express');
var args = require('minimist')(process.argv);

if(!args.u || !args.d || !args.p) {
    console.log('This example requires the ' +
    '-u (user), ' +
    '-d (mysql db) and ' +
    '-p (password) command line variables');

    process.exit();
}

var connection = mysql.createConnection({
    host     : 'localhost',
    user     : args.u,
    database : args.d,
    password : args.p,
    multipleStatements: true // This is so we can execute multiple statements
});
```

---

6. https://github.com/substack/minimist

```
connection.connect();

var app = express();

app.get('/', function (req, res) {
    res.send('ok');
});

app.get('/:name', function(req, res, next){

    // Query the account based on url parameters
    // As you can see we use no validation on the name parameter
    connection.query('SELECT * FROM accounts WHERE name="' + req.params.name + '"',
        function(err, rows, fields) {
            if (err) {
                next(err);
                return;
            }
            res.send(JSON.stringify(rows));
        });
});

app.listen(3000);
```

Let's ignore the fact that this application doesn't perform any user validation. You now have an application that displays the account information you requested via the name parameter in JSON format. The database dump would look like the following:

```
CREATE TABLE `accounts` (
    `id` int(11) NOT NULL AUTO_INCREMENT,
    `name` varchar(255) NOT NULL,
    `email` varchar(255) NOT NULL,
    PRIMARY KEY (`id`)
) ENGINE=InnoDB  DEFAULT CHARSET=utf8 AUTO_INCREMENT=3 ;

INSERT INTO `accounts` (`id`, `name`, `email`) VALUES
(1, 'karl', 'karl@dyyna.com'),
(2, 'juhan', 'juhan@gmail.com');
```

When you visit the URL /karl in the browser, you should see the following response:

```
[{
    "id": 1,
    "name": "karl",
    "email": "karl@dyyna.com"
}]
```

We could also construct the following URL to send the following SQL commands in a single line: /";SELECT%20*%20FROM%20accounts%20WHERE%20"1"="1. You can see here how the URL turns into two database queries:

```
SELECT * FROM accounts WHERE name="";SELECT * FROM accounts WHERE "1"="1;`
```

The first statement will return nothing because we didn't provide a value for name. However, the second statement will dump all the accounts stored in the database:

```
[
  [], // Our first query that selected nothing, since we terminated it
  [{
    "id": 1,
    "name": "karl",
    "email": "karl@dyyna.com"
  }, {
    "id": 2,
    "name": "juhan",
    "email": "juhan@gmail.com"
  }]
]
```

A select query is only the beginning of what we can do. Imagine the damage we could cause with /";DROP%20TABLE%20accounts;, which would delete the accounts table altogether. A database injection lets someone modify the commands sent to the database in order to view or modify the saved data. So how do you protect your application?

---

**Good News About Running Multiple Queries in MySQL**

The good news is that one of the most popular MySQL drivers for Node.js, node-mysql,[7] disables by default the ability to execute multiple commands in a single query. This makes SQL injection attacks much harder to launch on web applications if you use this module. The module won't let the attacker terminate the original query to start a separate malicious one. But for the sake of providing examples, we'll enable the multiple queries option in node-mysql.

## Avoid SQL Injection Attacks

As you just saw, attackers can cause a lot of damage with database injection. We'll now look at four main defense methods to protect against this kind of attack: controlled error messages, input validation, escaping, and prepared statements.

---

7. https://github.com/felixge/node-mysql

Database injection attacks are divided into two types: blind and normal SQL injection. In normal SQL injection the attacker will see helpful error messages and/or the result of the attack on the web page. With blind SQL injection, the attacker sees only generic error messages if something is not valid.

In case of blind SQL injection attackers frequently append true-false statements such as `and 1=2` or `and 1=1` at the end of the query to see the different messages associated with successful and unsuccessful attempts. Blind SQL injection requires the attacker to collect the information needed one piece at a time.

The mechanics of defending are the same, but blind SQL injection is much harder and more time consuming for the attacker to pull off. This is why your first line of defense is to handle errors properly, as previously discussed in *Limit Error Messages in Production*, on page 18. Forcing the attacker to spend more time determining whether there is a vulnerability and how to get at the data benefits you.

The second step is validating user input. You'll have to verify that user-entered data falls within expected parameters and is not malicious. Say you're manually constructing MySQL commands by combining user-entered data with queries hardcoded within the application code. This approach is very important if you're using a database driver and handling database queries this way. You have to be attentive when checking every input to make sure users aren't entering malicious strings. The best approach is *whitelisting*, or allowing only types of data you expect to see.

Let's go back to the previous example and see how you can validate user input:

```
chp-5-database/mysql-exploitable-validation.js
var connection = mysql.createConnection({
    host     : 'localhost',
    user     : args.u,
    database : args.d,
    password : args.p,
    multipleStatements: true // This is so we can execute multiple statements
});
connection.connect();

var app = express();

app.get('/', function (req, res) {
    res.send('ok');
});
```

```
app.get('/:name', function(req, res, next){
    // Validate that the name has only letters
    if(req.params.name.match(/[^a-zA-Z]/)) {
        // It didn't so send a Bad Request response
        res.sendStatus(400);
        return;
    }

    // Query the account based on url parameters
    connection.query('SELECT * FROM accounts WHERE name="' + req.params.name + '"',
        function(err, rows, fields) {
            if (err) {
                next(err);
                return;
            }
            res.send(JSON.stringify(rows));
        });
});
```

This is restrictive but efficient. The thing is, you can't take this approach all the time because you don't always have such a clear understanding of what would be considered valid input.

Let's move on to the third approach, escaping. This means that all characters that can potentially break the query are formatted in such a way that the application doesn't treat them as part of a command.

This is a widely used method and many libraries, including node-mysql, provide ready-to-go functions for escaping well-known problem characters. You can utilize connection.escape(), which is the Node equivalent of PHP's mysqli_escape_string(). This way you don't have the hassle of trying to write the function yourself since you can just use a well-tested one.

So modify your vulnerable example again to escape the input string:

chp-5-database/mysql-exploitable-fixed.js
```
var connection = mysql.createConnection({
    host     : 'localhost',
    user     : args.u,
    database : args.d,
    password : args.p,
    multipleStatements: true // This is so we can execute multiple statements
});
connection.connect();

var app = express();

app.get('/', function (req, res) {
    res.send('ok');
});
```

```
app.get('/:name', function(req, res, next){
➤    // Query the account based on url parameters
➤    var query = 'SELECT * FROM accounts WHERE name="' +
➤        connection.escape(req.params.name) + '"';
➤
➤    connection.query(query, function(err, rows, fields) {
        if (err) {
            next(err);
            return;
        }
        res.send(JSON.stringify(rows));
    });
});
```

The previous attack string no longer works because the quotation marks are escaped. The application now knows the quotes should be treated as part of a string and not as part of a command.

The final method is to use prepared statements; see the following illustration. Here, you completely separate the command and data parts of the query by sending them to the database separately. This leaves no room for misinterpretation and is a good way to protect against injection. As a bonus, it also provides a speed boost on queries that run many times because you can reuse the same procedure.

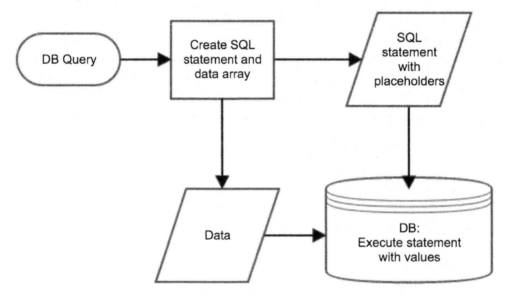

Try out this technique:

```
chp-5-database/mysql-exploitable-fixed-prep.js
var connection = mysql.createConnection({
    host     : 'localhost',
    user     : args.u,
    database : args.d,
    password : args.p,
    multipleStatements: true // This is so we can execute multiple statements
});
connection.connect();

var app = express();

app.get('/', function (req, res) {
    res.send('ok');
});

app.get('/:name', function(req, res, next){

    // Query the account based on url parameters
    connection.query('SELECT * FROM accounts WHERE name= ?', [req.params.name],
        function(err, rows, fields) {
            if (err) {
                next(err);
                return;
            }
            res.send(JSON.stringify(rows));
        });
});
```

Prepared statements are by far the best solution against SQL injection attacks and are the favored approach. The second-best option is to use proper escaping, which is the method node-mysql uses currently. Whitelisting, while very effective, is the least favored. That's because it's time consuming to whitelist all possible endpoints and sometimes you need to have special characters in the query, which makes this approach less effective. Whichever method you use in your application, don't forget to limit the error messages.

---

**Prepared like node-mysql**

 While you can use prepared statement syntax with node-mysql, such syntax is internally executed using connection.escape() and is not prepared statements. node-mysql2[8] is a library that does support prepared statements, and hopefully they will soon be available in node-mysql as well.

---

8.   https://github.com/sidorares/node-mysql2

Now that you know the three ways to protect yourself when constructing database commands, you can feel confident that you aren't such an easy target for attackers. You might be able to order that Tesla after all.

## Watch Out for Sneaky Issues

Before you start patting yourself on the back for a job well done, you still have a few hurdles left to address. Developers often use an ORM (object-relational mapper) instead of constructing commands manually, and that can introduce some unexpected behavior.

Numerous ORMs are available for Node.js and various databases. Let's look at one of the popular ORM mappers for MySQL, MariaDB, SQLite, and Post-greSQL in Node.js—Sequelize.[9] While ORMs typically implement internal escaping based on model properties and types, Sequelize does not always perform thorough input cleaning. Some inputs are left vulnerable and can be used to construct malicious SQL statements. It would be foolish to assume the ORM is going to do something without checking. Trust but verify.

ORMs by their nature introduce overhead into your application, because they construct interfaces around your data structures. This can lead to serious performance issues in some cases. So using an ORM isn't always the best solution. But if you're going to use ORMs, you need to test how they handle input cleaning. We will look at Sequelize.

First, let's do the setup:

chp-5-database/sequelize-example.js
```
'use strict';

var express = require('express');
var Sequelize = require('sequelize');
var args = require('minimist')(process.argv);

if(!args.u || !args.d || !args.p) {
    console.log('This example requires the ' +
    '-u (user), ' +
    '-d (mysql db) and ' +
    '-p (password) command line variables');

    process.exit();
}

// Define connection to DB
var sequelize = new Sequelize(args.d, args.u, args.p, {
```

---

9.   http://sequelizejs.com/

```
    dialect: 'mysql',
    port:    3306
});

// Define user model
var User = sequelize.define('user', {
    company: Sequelize.STRING,
    username: Sequelize.STRING
});
```

Now that we've done the database connection part, let's define the application paths:

chp-5-database/sequelize-example.js

```
var app = express();

app.get('/', function (req, res) {
    res.send('ok');
});

// Define a path where we can ask users by
// company name and optionally limit the response
app.get('/:company/:limit*?', function(req, res, next){

    console.log(req.params);
    User.findAll({
        where: {
            company: req.params.company
        },
        limit: req.params.limit || 0
    }).then(function(users) {
        res.send(JSON.stringify(users));
    }).catch(next);
});
```

Finally, we create our example database entries and set the ball rolling:

chp-5-database/sequelize-example.js

```
// Set up the database
sequelize
    .authenticate()
    .then(function() {
        // Sync the models
        return sequelize.sync({ force: true });
    })
    .then(function () {
        // Push example data into the database
        return User.bulkCreate([
            { username: 'karl', company: 'nodeswat' },
            { username: 'harri', company: 'nodeswat' },
            { username: 'jaanus', company: 'nodeswat' },
```

```
            { username: 'jaak', company: 'mektro' }
        ]).then(function() {
            // We are set up so start listening
            app.listen(3000);
        });
    })
    .catch(function (err) {
        console.log('Unable to connect to the database:', err)
        process.exit();
    });
```

Now when we send the URL /nodeswat we should get the following data dump:

```
[{
    "id": 1,
    "company": "nodeswat",
    "username": "karl",
    "createdAt": "2014-01-24T11:33:01.000Z",
    "updatedAt": "2014-01-24T11:33:01.000Z"
}, {
    "id": 2,
    "company": "nodeswat",
    "username": "harri",
    "createdAt": "2014-01-24T11:33:01.000Z",
    "updatedAt": "2014-01-24T11:33:01.000Z"
}, {
    "id": 3,
    "company": "nodeswat",
    "username": "jaanus",
    "createdAt": "2014-01-24T11:33:01.000Z",
    "updatedAt": "2014-01-24T11:33:01.000Z"
}]
```

Let's take a look at the actual database command that was executed. So far, so good:

```
SELECT * FROM `users` WHERE `users`.`company`='nodeswat';
```

When we add in malicious code as shown in the following URL, /nodeswat"';, we see that the quotation marks are properly escaped (as expected!):

```
SELECT * FROM `users` WHERE `users`.`company`='nodeswat\'\";';
```

When we use the limit parameter in the URL like /nodeswat/1;DROP%20TABLE%20users, we get an error. But let's look at the final command that was constructed. As you can see, this could have gone badly:

```
SELECT * FROM `users` WHERE `users`.`company`='nodeswat' LIMIT 1;DROP TABLE users;
```

The only reason the command didn't execute and drop the users table was that Sequelize uses node-mysql as its MySQL driver. As you saw earlier, node-mysql disables by default the ability to run multiple statements off a single command. But PostgreSQL's driver doesn't have that setting, so a similar attack will succeed on that database. You'll need to do validation or change the configuration if you're working with PostgreSQL or other databases that don't disable multiple queries by default:

```
var sequelize = new Sequelize(args.d, args.u, args.p, {
    dialect: 'postgres',
    port: 5432
});
```

Here, the solution is to either not allow the user to set the limit parameter or validate that you're dealing with a number.

The moral of this example is that you must be ever vigilant when using third-party modules and talking to the database. You should always limit user interaction with your database and test what users are allowed to do. Knowing this makes you security conscious and in a better position to write secure applications.

## Mitigate Injection Attacks in NoSQL Databases

MongoDB and CouchDB[10] are widely used alternatives to relational databases when building Node.js applications. They don't use a query language like SQL for mapping the data—hence the name NoSQL. Instead they have their own methods and queries. You may now think that using NoSQL means SQL injection is not a problem for you. Alas, that isn't quite true.

Strictly speaking, SQL injection doesn't affect NoSQL databases. The thing is, SQL injection isn't the only form of database injection, and there are other ways to inject commands despite not using the traditional SQL syntax. These NoSQL injection attacks execute within a procedural language rather than in the declarative SQL language, so the potential impact of these attacks is greater.

In the following examples we'll be using MongoDB,[11] since it's the most popular NoSQL database in use with Node.js.

The first security issue for NoSQL databases is that by default they don't have any authentication. Instead, they filter connections only to localhost. As you saw in *Start with the Basics: Set Up the Database*, on page 54, that's not necessarily a good thing.

---

10. http://couchdb.apache.org/
11. http://www.mongodb.org

Let's see how to connect to our configured MongoDB using a password with one of the most (if not the most) popular MongoDB ORMs in use—Mongoose:[12]

```
mongoose.connect('mongodb://user:pass@localhost:port/database');
```

The following example uses mongoose and express to illustrate how MongoDB can be susceptible to attack:

```
chp-5-database/mongoose-example.js
'use strict';

var express = require('express');
var mongoose = require('mongoose');
var args = require('minimist')(process.argv);

if(!args.d) {
    console.log('This example requires the -d (mongoose db) command line variable');
    process.exit();
}

// Connect to mongoose db
mongoose.connect(args.d);
mongoose.connection.on('error', function (err) {
    console.error('connection error:' + err);
    process.exit();
});

// Define user model
var userSchema = new mongoose.Schema({
    username:  { type: String, required: true, index: { unique: true } },
    company: { type: String, required: true },
    age: { type: Number, required: true}
});
var User = mongoose.model('User', userSchema);

User.remove().exec(); // Delete all previous Users.

var app = express();

app.get('/', function(req, res){
    res.send('ok');
});

app.get('/:age', function (req, res, next) {
    // Lets implement a completely unvalidated way to query the documents
    User.find({ $where: 'this.age < ' + req.params.age }, function (err, users) {
        if(err) {
            next(err);
```

---

12. http://mongoosejs.com/

```
                return;
            }
            res.send(JSON.stringify(users));
        });
    });
});
// Fill database
User.create([
    { username: 'karl', company: 'nodeswat', age: 25 },
    { username: 'harri', company: 'nodeswat', age: 35 },
    { username: 'jaanus', company: 'nodeswat', age: 45 },
    { username: 'jaak', company: 'mektro', age: 55 }
], function (err) {
    if(err) {
        console.error(err);
        process.exit(1);
    }
    console.log('Listening');
    app.listen(3000);
});
```

With this application, you can ask for a list of users under a specific age. Constructing a URL with /40 would result in a data dump of some users:

```
[{
    "username": "karl",
    "company": "nodeswat",
    "age": 25,
    "_id": "52e25cc4251a7ce88b050e75",
    "__v": 0
}, {
    "username": "harri",
    "company": "nodeswat",
    "age": 35,
    "_id": "52e25cc4251a7ce88b050e76",
    "__v": 0
}]
```

The user input was not validated before constructing the search, which means attackers can add malicious code into the statement. MongoDB won't be affected by SQL statements, but it does support JavaScript commands in its queries. The attacker can execute JavaScript statements on the database layer. It may look something like this URL, which would trigger a ten-second loop in the database:

/40;var%20date=new%20Date();%20do%7BcurDate%20=%20new%20Date();%7Dwhile(curDate-date<10000);

Keep in mind that this is a simple example; the attacker has access to the whole JavaScript syntax to craft a more complicated query. Because most

NoSQL databases don't support prepared statements, you're left with two solutions—validation and escaping. Be sure to use them liberally.

You just saw that NoSQL is not inherently safer just because it does not have SQL. When constructing complex queries with user input, make sure the data falls within the narrowly defined parameters of your query, just as you would with a SQL database.

## Wrapping Up

Databases are an integral and powerful part of a web application, and you must secure all transactions in order to protect your clients' data. As you learned in this chapter, you must secure your database connections and limit access privileges where you can. You must also be vigilant about escaping and validating all user input that comes into contact with the database, even if it's a NoSQL database. Implementing these two steps will greatly increase the security of your data.

Now that you've secured how the application communicates with the database, the attackers will find it harder to target your application. Don't get too cozy just yet, because there are many more attack vectors to defeat out there. Next we'll move on to another common issue in web application design that also affects databases: concurrency. Let's go.

*Time is what we want most, but what we use worst.*

> ➤ *William Penn*

# CHAPTER 6

# Learn to Do Things Concurrently

You've learned a lot about different ways to secure your configuration and communications so that attackers wouldn't be able to introduce malicious variables into your code. In this chapter, we take a slight detour and study application design, specifically, *concurrency*.

Concurrency has been a problem in application design since the beginning of parallel computing. Two processes running modifications on the same resource can cause a number of different issues. This is not technically a security issue because the user isn't circumventing a specific security measure, but it still poses serious security-related issues. In fact, if you're aware of how millions of bitcoins were stolen from the Mt. Gox exchange last year, then you should know the thieves did so by abusing concurrency issues. It's a real-world problem, and we're going to devote some time to it in this chapter so that you can avoid the same fate.

We'll start by identifying concurrency issues and learning how they occur and then see how you can avoid those problems while keeping your application intact. While this may feel like basic computer science material to many of you, it will be a good reminder of how the topic applies to web security.

## A Primer on Concurrency Issues

Problems of concurrency happen when multiple application processes modify and use the same resource at the same time, or concurrently. Process state mutates unexpectedly, leading to double processing and other issues. Problems tend to occur when the resource is being accessed within a short timespan, as shown in the following diagram, but it can also happen over a longer period.

**Two processes withdrawing 100 from the same account at the same time**

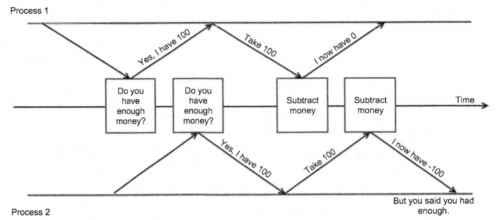

Technically, concurrency issues aren't constrained to the database layer, but they most often occur there because the database is the typically the most shared resource.

Although we treat concurrency and parallelism as synonyms in this chapter, you should be aware that they're different. *Concurrency* refers to when two tasks either start, run, or complete in overlapping time periods, as would happen on a single-core machine. They don't have to run at the same instant. *Parallelism* refers to when tasks literally run at the same time, such as on a multi-core processor.

While talking about Node.js we mostly talk about concurrency when dealing with a single thread and overlapping async processes. When we fork into multiple threads on a multi-core machine, then we can start talking about parallelism as a separate concept.

Let me illustrate this complicated explanation with an example you're likely to be familiar with: a withdrawal system for a wallet in an e-commerce application. The application shows how much money you currently have in your wallet and lets you withdraw some money.

First, we set up the models:

```
chp-6-concurrency/concurrency-wallet-mongo.js
var mongoose = require('mongoose');
var args = require('minimist')(process.argv);

if(!args.d) {
    console.log('This example requires the -d (mongoose db) command line variable');
    process.exit();
}
```

```
// Connect to mongoose db
mongoose.connect(args.d);
mongoose.connection.on('error', function (err) {
    console.error('connection error:' + err);
    process.exit();
});

// Define wallet model
var walletSchema = new mongoose.Schema({
    name:   { type: String, required: true, index: { unique: true } },
    amount: { type: Number, required: true}
});
var Wallet = mongoose.model('Wallet', walletSchema);

Wallet.remove().exec(); // Delete all previous Wallets.
```

The access points let us see and manipulate the data in the database:

chp-6-concurrency/concurrency-wallet-mongo.js
```
var bodyParser = require('body-parser');
var express = require('express');
var app = express();
app.use(bodyParser.urlencoded({extended: false}));

app.get('/:name', function(req, res, next){
    // Query the account based on url parameters
    Wallet.findOne({name: req.params.name}, function(err, wallet) {
        if (err) {
            next(err);
            return;
        }
        // Send information and withdrawal form
        res.send(
            '<p> You have: ' + wallet.amount + '.<br/>' +
            'How much do you want to withdraw?</p>' +
            '<form method="POST">' +
            '<input type="number" name="amount" />' +
            '<input type="submit" value="submit" />' +
            '</form>');
    });
});

app.post('/:name', function(req, res, next){
    var amount = Math.abs(req.body.amount);

    Wallet.findOne({name: req.params.name}, function (err, wallet) {
        if (err) { // Something went wrong with the query
            next(err);
            return;
        }
        if(!wallet) {
```

```
            res.send(404, 'Not found');
            return;
        }
        if(wallet.amount < amount) {
            res.send(400, 'Insufficient funds');
            return;
        }
        wallet.amount -= amount;
        wallet.save(function (rErr, updatedW, rowsAffected) {
            if(rErr || rowsAffected !== 1) {
                res.send(500, 'Withdrawal failed');
                return;
            }
            res.redirect('/' + req.params.name);
        });
    });
});
```

We then fill the database with some test data:

chp-6-concurrency/concurrency-wallet-mongo.js
```
// Fill database
Wallet.create([
    { name: 'karl', amount: 1000},
    { name: 'mikk', amount: 1000}
], function (err) {
    if(err) {
        console.error(err);
        process.exit(1);
    }
    console.log('Listening');
    app.listen(3000);
});
```

In order to induce concurrency issues, you'd normally have to make multiple requests close to each other, but that's difficult to demonstrate. So let's add a processing function to the application to mimic the request to a bank for the money transfer. To further simplify the demonstration, let's make the time period five seconds.

chp-6-concurrency/concurrency-wallet-mongo-delay.js
```
➤ // Our processing function
➤ function processCall(cb) {
➤     // Add delay of 5 seconds here - imitating processing of the request
➤     setTimeout(cb, 5000);
➤ }

app.post('/:name', function(req, res, next){
    var amount = Math.abs(req.body.amount);
```

```
Wallet.findOne({name: req.params.name}, function (err, wallet) {
    if (err) { // Something went wrong with the query
        next(err);
        return;
    }
    if(!wallet) {
        res.send(404, 'Not found');
        return;
    }
    if(wallet.amount < amount) {
        res.send(400, 'Insufficient funds');
        return;
    }
    processCall(function () {
        wallet.amount -= amount;
        wallet.save(function (rErr, updatedW, rowsAffected) {
            if(rErr || rowsAffected !== 1) {
                res.send(500, 'Withdrawal failed');
                return;
            }
            res.redirect('/' + req.params.name);
        });
    });
});
```

Now we have two accounts with 1000 starting money and the ability to withdraw some of it. If we make a request to withdraw 300, then in a little while we'll see only 700 in our wallet and 300 in our account. But if we make two requests at the same time to withdraw 300, we'll see both processes go through. However, we'll wind up with 700 still in our wallet instead of the 400 we'd expect to see. We just made 300 out of thin air.

You see, both processes looked up the wallet's amount in the database and got 1000. Both processes deducted 300 and saved the resulting value of 700 back to the database. If the second process starts before the first one finishes writing the new value back to the database, it will use the wrong amount in its calculations.

In the Mt. Gox robbery, this is exactly what happened. With enough concurrent requests, the system lost integrity and paid out more bitcoins—millions of dollars worth—than it was supposed to. You don't want this to happen to you, so let's see how you can avoid this in your application.

## Ways to Mitigate Concurrency

The underlying problem is multiple processes working on the same resource, so the mitigation methods look at how to limit exposure. Let's first look at general concepts and then look more specifically at databases, which usually are at the heart of concurrency issues.

Two simple generic methods, resource locks and atomic operations, are generally good enough to use in most situations. Locking deals directly with concurrency by preventing simultaneous process flows. Atomic operations move operations closer to the resources and enforce serialization at the resource level.

Locking the resources so no one else can run them makes sense if the workflow is not supposed to run concurrently. In the withdrawal example, you wouldn't want the same person to make multiple concurrent operations. The following flowchart illustrates how locks work. You start by having the process acquire a lock. If it fails, another process is already using the resource and it must wait for that process to finish. If the lock acquiring succeeds, you process the request. After you finish, you release the lock.

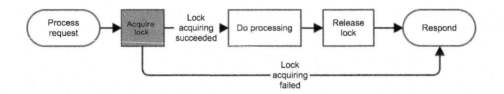

The process seems straightforward, but there are a few problems with this kind of resource locking. The locking process itself must be atomic and not subject to concurrency issues. You don't want to lock up the whole table, so you have to make sure the lock only affects a small area of the application. There also needs to be a fail-safe in case the process fails to unlock a resource or the program crashes before the locks are released.

Locking creates bottlenecks in applications, and so it's not recommended if you need high throughput, if the process affects a large part of the resouces, or processing takes a long time. You want the lock to be in place over a small area for a short period of time. Otherwise, you should modify the application logic or use atomic operations instead.

Atomic operations address concurrency by moving operations closer to the resource and in a manner that prevents other processes from manipulating data in between operations. Some operations are truly atomic. They tend to be simple functions that run serially in the resource layer, such as INSERT in SQL and INCR in Redis. When this command is running, another one won't run against the same table during that time.

Some operations can be grouped and performed as an atomic operation, such as MULTI in Redis. Several commands are grouped together and executed as a block without allowing other operations while they're running. Other operations are optimistic locks, such as TRANSACTION in SQL and WATCH EXEC in Redis. They tend to be used for more complex tasks and involve executing the operations as a sequence. If no errors occur and no other process has modified the same resources during the execution of the sequence, then all the operations will be run and committed. If something goes wrong, the rollback restores state to what it was before the transaction started.

Atomic operations modify the resource serially by not allowing other operations to access the resource during that time. At a close level they can and sometimes are implemented with lock mechanisms. Only the locking processing and unlocking happen in a short timespan and inside the operation.

## Concurrency with MongoDB Explained

Let's move back to practical usage and look at MongoDB since it's the most used NoSQL database for Node.js applications.

MongoDB doesn't guarantee ACID compliance[1] in all cases. For example, MongoDB doesn't have transactions and atomic functions that cover multiple documents. So if you have a database model where you need to avoid concurrency issues with multiple documents at the same time, you're in trouble. For example, you might have an e-commerce application that needs to decrement the number of products in the warehouse inventory while at the same time withdrawing money from the user's wallet.

Faced with this situation you are left the option to modify the database schema to collect information into single documents so that you can use atomic functions, or you can create a locking mechanism for a collection of documents. MongoDB has good information in its documentation about two-phase commit,[2] which is essentially a locking mechanism. Finally, you could also use another database, either in conjunction with MongoDB or completely migrate to that.

---

1.   http://stackoverflow.com/questions/7149890/what-does-mongodb-not-being-acid-compliant-really-mean

2.   http://docs.mongodb.org/manual/tutorial/perform-two-phase-commits/

## ACID Compliance

When talking about concurrency and databases, the first thing that's usually looked at is whether the database is ACID compliant. That doesn't mean it must be able to withstand an acid attack; rather *ACID* stands for "Atomicity, Consistency, Isolation, Durability."

What these mean:

- Atomicity: operations must be atomic.
- Consistency: every transaction must leave the database in a consistent (valid) state.
- Isolation: transactions cannot interfere with each other.
- Durability: effects of transactions must persist through crashes.

The reasoning is that concurrency issues are far easier to deal with in an ACID-compliant database.

---

**Mongo vs. Other**

I think this is a good spot to point out that *just because you're using Node.js in your application, it doesn't mean that a NoSQL database is the best solution for you*—database selection should be determined by your application and information types and connections.

In this section, we'll fix the example using locks and atomic functions. Locking is the more general solution because you can extend it over several operations and more complex applications; this specific example benefits more from atomic functions. So let's look at the simpler atomic approach and then see how you can use locking.

To use atomic functions we need to modify our logic to deduct the amount first and then perform the operation. If anything goes wrong, we reimburse the amount:

```
chp-6-concurrency/concurrency-wallet-mongo-delay-atomic.js
// Our processing function
function processCall(cb) {
    // Add delay of 5 seconds here - imitating processing of the request
    setTimeout(cb, 5000);
}

app.post('/:name', function(req, res, next){
    var amount = Math.abs(req.body.amount);

    // Search by name and amount greater than or equal to requested
    var search = {name: req.params.name, amount: {$gte: amount}};
```

```
      // Increment by negative amount
      var update = {$inc: {amount: -amount}};
      Wallet.findOneAndUpdate(search, update, function (err, wallet) {
          if (err) { // Something went wrong with the query
              next(err);
              return;
          }
          if(!wallet) {
              res.send(400, 'Insufficient funds or not found');
              return;
          }

          processCall(function (err) {
              if(err) {
                  // Process failed so reimburse
                  wallet.amount += amount;
                  wallet.save(function (rErr, updatedW, rowsAffected) {
                      if(rErr || rowsAffected !== 1) {
                          //TODO: This needs careful handling
                          console.error('Reimbursement failed');
                      }
                      res.send(500);
                  });
                  return;
              }
              res.redirect('/' + req.params.name);
          });
      });
  });
```

And with these simple modifications our application is secure against concurrency attacks. All the calculations are atomic and the results will be correct.

Now let's expand our database model to include a lock model so that you can see how to achieve the same thing with locking:

chp-6-concurrency/concurrency-wallet-mongo-delay-lock.js
```
var mongoose = require('mongoose');
var args = require('minimist')(process.argv);

if(!args.d) {
    console.log('This example requires the -d (mongoose db) command line variable');
    process.exit();
}

// Connect to mongoose db
mongoose.connect(args.d);
mongoose.connection.on('error', function (err) {
    console.error('connection error:' + err);
    process.exit();
});
```

```
// Define wallet model
var walletSchema = new mongoose.Schema({
    name:   { type: String, required: true, index: { unique: true } },
    amount: { type: Number, required: true}
});
var Wallet = mongoose.model('Wallet', walletSchema);

// Define wallet model
var lockSchema = new mongoose.Schema({
    name:   { type: String, required: true, index: { unique: true } }
});
var Lock = mongoose.model('Lock', lockSchema);

Wallet.remove().exec(); // Delete all previous Wallets.
```

At this point, we'll create and apply the mechanism to lock the resources and release them afterward:

```
chp-6-concurrency/concurrency-wallet-mongo-delay-lock.js
// Our processing function
function processCall(cb) {
    // Add delay of 5 seconds here - imitating processing of the request
    setTimeout(cb, 5000);
}

function aquireLock(name, cb) {
    // We will use the fact that name is unique and
    // so insert will fail if a lock exists
    Lock.create({ name: name }, function (err, lock) {
        if(err) {
            cb(new Error('Failed to aquire lock'));
            return;
        }
        cb(null, lock);
    });
}

function releaseLock(name, cb) {
    Lock.findOneAndRemove({name: name}, cb);
}

app.post('/:name', function(req, res, next){
    var amount = Math.abs(req.body.amount);

    aquireLock(req.params.name, function (err) {
        if(err) {
            res.send(409, 'Already processing');
            return;
        }
        Wallet.findOne({name: req.params.name}, function (err, wallet) {
```

```
        if (err) { // Something went wrong with the query
            next(err);
            return;
        }
        if(!wallet) {
            res.send(404, 'Not found');
            return;
        }
        if(wallet.amount < amount) {
            res.send(400, 'Insufficient funds');
            return;
        }
        processCall(function () {
            wallet.amount -= amount;
            wallet.save(function (rErr, updatedW, rowsAffected) {
                if(rErr || rowsAffected !== 1) {
                    res.send(500, 'Withdrawal failed');
                    return;
                }
                releaseLock(req.params.name, function (err) {
                    if(err) {
                        //FIXME: We should definitely handle the error here
                        console.error(err);
                    }
                    res.redirect('/' + req.params.name);
                });
            });
        });
    });
});
```

We can acquire a lock atomically to the wallet and perform operations before releasing the lock. Because this example doesn't take into account any potential errors, we can wind up with eternally locked resources. We'll solve that problem by adding a timeout to the lock:

**chp-6-concurrency/concurrency-wallet-mongo-delay-lock-improved.js**
```
// Define wallet model
var lockSchema = new mongoose.Schema({
    name:  { type: String, required: true, index: { unique: true } },
    timestamp: {type: Number}
});
var Lock = mongoose.model('Lock', lockSchema);
```

Now when acquiring the lock, we'll have to adjust for the timestamp to prevent eternal locks:

```
chp-6-concurrency/concurrency-wallet-mongo-delay-lock-improved.js
// Our processing function
function processCall(cb) {
    // Add delay of 5 seconds here - imitating processing of the request
    setTimeout(cb, 5000);
}

function aquireLock(name, cb) {
    var now = Date.now();
    var expired = now - 60 * 1000;

    // The basics of this command is that we either:
    // 1. Find an old lock and update it with a new timestamp
    // 2. Don't find one, in which case we try to insert
    //     This will either:
    //     2.1 fail, because of unique index - a lock exists
    //     2.2 succeeds - a new lock is created
    Lock.findOneAndUpdate({
        name: name,
        timestamp: {$lt: expired} //Include locks that are too old
    }, {
        timestamp: now
    }, {
        'new': true,    // return new doc if one is upserted
        upsert: true // insert the document if it does not exist
    }, function (err, lock) {
        if(err) {
            cb(new Error('Failed to aquire lock'));
            return;
        }
        cb(null, lock);
    });
}


function releaseLock(name, cb) {
    Lock.findOneAndRemove({name: name}, cb);
}
```

Both of these solutions are valid. Atomic functions require you to change your operational logic only slightly, but you can see that locking mechanisms are more versatile.

## Concurrency with MySQL Explained

SQL databases such as MySQL are more mature than NoSQL when it comes to concurrency and ACID compliance. All the solutions we just covered in *Concurrency with MongoDB Explained*, on page 79 also apply to MySQL. Only the database query syntax is different.

However, MySQL also has transactions,[3] which means that you can do ACID-compliant operations over multiple tables. This means you can solve the problem of updating multiple tables atomically in SQL databases.

Let's continue with our previous warehouse and wallet example. We won't construct a full example because that would introduce too much overhead. Instead we'll just highlight the way you would check the product out of the warehouse and into the shopping cart as part of a single transaction:

```
chp-6-concurrency/concurrency-mysql-transaction.js
// First we start the transaction
connection.beginTransaction(function(err) {
    if (err) {
        next(err);
        return;
    }
    // Then we remove items from warehouse
    var warehouseSql = 'UPDATE warehouse SET quantity = quantity - ? ' +
        'WHERE quantity >= ? AND id = ?';

    connection.query(warehouseSql, [quantity, quantity, productId],
        function(wErr, result) {
            if (wErr) {
                // Unsuccessful so rollback
                connection.rollback(function() {
                    next(wErr);
                });
                return;
            }

            if(result.changedRows !== 1) { // Not enough items in warehouse
                connection.rollback(function() {
                    res.send(400, 'Insufficient funds');
                });
                return;
            }

            // Add items to cart
            var cartSql = 'UPDATE wallets ' +
                'SET amount = amount - ? WHERE amount >= ? AND name = ?';

            connection.query(cartSql, [amount, amount, name],
                function(cErr) {
                    if (cErr) {
                        // Unsuccessful so rollback
                        connection.rollback(function() {
                            next(cErr);
```

---

3.    http://dev.mysql.com/doc/refman/5.5/en/commit.html

```
            });
            return;
        }
        // We have updated both so commit the result
        connection.commit(function(commitErr) {
            if (commitErr) {
                connection.rollback(function() {
                    next(commitErr);
                });
                return;
            }
            // Everything went successfully
            res.send(200);
        });
    });
  });
});
```

This code makes those two queries inside a transaction—if you fail at any point, then you roll back the whole thing and no unwanted changes are left in the database.

## Wrapping Up

In this chapter we looked at how concurrency issues occur and how they can cause big problems if the application logic doesn't account for it. You learned how to mitigate concurrency by denying other processes access to a resource until one process is finished by using locks. You also learned how to work with atomic operations, where you implement changes to the resource as part of a single operation. You should now know how to handle concurrent operations in MongoDB and MySQL.

Next, we look at ways to limit access to different resources. In the next chapter, we get cracking on building the backbone of our authentication scheme.

*If you know the enemy and know yourself, you need not fear the result of a hundred battles.*

> ➤ *Sun Tzu*

# CHAPTER 7

# Bring Authentication to Your Application

You've securely set up your server and database, and you now have an application with valuable information people want to see. But how do you know a user is who he or she claims to be, and how do you avoid malicious impersonators? You don't want to hand out personal information to just anyone, so you need to think about authentication.

The level of security you need when dealing with user accounts and how to validate them depends on the application and how much personal information you're storing. Consider how much damage an attacker can do to the customer if the account is breached. If the application stores credit card information, then it must have extra levels of validation to protect users and their data. This chapter focuses on the common username/password authentication system because you're already familiar with it and because it's easy to understand.

**Don't Forget About PCI DSS if You Store Credit Cards**

 When dealing with credit card information, you have to follow the Payment Card Industry Data Security Standard (PCI DSS).[1]

A user sets up an account by providing a secret (a password), and later you verify that the user knows the secret before allowing access. Controlling this knowledge lets you assume that you're dealing with a trusted party. But because everyone uses this form of authentication, there are many attack vectors that specifically attempt to break it.

We'll look at various parts of this system and how to harden your setup so it will be more robust and not easily fooled.

---

1. https://www.pcisecuritystandards.org/security_standards/

## Store the Secret in a Safe Place

Let's start with storage—you have to store the password somewhere so that you can validate that the user knows the secret. There's a big difference between saving the password and saving the password *securely*.

First off, and I do hope I stress this enough, *never, ever store passwords in plain text*. That's just asking for trouble. You may think that people who will see the passwords will already have access to the data—so what's the big deal. Oh, how wrong you would be.

There are two important differences between storing passwords in plain text and hashed: impersonation and collateral damage. First off, seeing the password in hashed format will not allow you to simply log in as the user because you still don't know the secret. Depriving a malicious party of this is already a big win; however, the bigger issue is your users themselves. People tend to reuse passwords on different sites—so knowing a user's password on one site potentially gives access to several other accounts on other sites as well.

If you store passwords in plain text on the disk, then you're both putting an awful lot of trust in your administrations and gambling with your users' data, since even a simple breach in your security will allow the attacker to compromise not only your site but likely other accounts on other sites as well. So do everyone a favor and say no to plain text.

Plain text is the worst choice you can make. But if you were thinking about using general-purpose hash functions such as MD5, SHA1, SHA256, SHA512, and SHA-3, then you would also be wrong. They're designed to calculate the hash as fast as possible, a feature you don't want in a password-hashing function. You want the attackers to have to spend a long time trying to crack the hashes in case of a database breach.

### Why Passwords Get Cracked

Let me digress to discuss cracking for a moment. If the application stores its passwords in hash format, attackers who get their hands on the hashes can't use the hash directly to log into the application. They need to find a plain-text version of the password. This gets harder if the password is stored using one-way hashing functions. Then the only way to determine the original password is to generate hashes for all possiblities until they find a matching one. How fast the function can calculate the hash has a significant impact on password safety.

A modern server can calculate an MD5 hash of about 330 MB every second. This means that if you have lowercase, alphanumeric passwords that are six characters long, then every possible combination can be calculated in 40 seconds. That's without investing any real money. If attackers are willing to pay, they can drastically increase computational power and reduce the time required to crack hashes. Also, sometimes flaws are discovered in the hashing algorithm itself that help narrow the possible inputs, greatly decreasing the time it takes to find a solution.

Attackers take the time and effort to crack the passwords because they can go after other user accounts on the current site as well as any place the passwords may have been reused.

"Hey, but I salt my passwords!" you may be saying right now. Well, salts won't help if the attackers are intent on cracking your passwords. Salts were designed to defend against dictionary attacks, but computational power is so cheap nowadays that attackers just go straight to brute-force cracking.

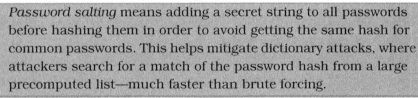

**Salting**

*Password salting* means adding a secret string to all passwords before hashing them in order to avoid getting the same hash for common passwords. This helps mitigate dictionary attacks, where attackers search for a match of the password hash from a large precomputed list—much faster than brute forcing.

## Use Hash Functions Designed for Passwords

With the quick lesson in cracking, you should now know why general hash functions aren't recommended for passwords. Instead, use *bcrypt*[2] or *scrypt*,[3] which are specifically designed for passwords.

bcrypt is based on the Blowfish[4] cipher and is slow in hash calculation depending on the number of iterations. scrypt was developed to make it costly to perform custom hardware attacks by raising the memory requirements of the hash calculation, thus increasing the cost of hardware implementations.

Let's see how these compare to each other on my laptop. In my code I used the most popular bcrypt[5] and scrypt[6] libraries for Node.js. Using twelve iterations

2.  http://bcrypt.sourceforge.net
3.  https://www.scrypt.com
4.  https://www.schneier/com/blowfish.com
5.  https://github.com/ncb000gt/node.bcrypt.js
6.  https://github.com/barrysteyn/node-scrypt

on bcrypt and the default settings for scrypt (with max calculation time of 1s) I got the following results:

```
    md5: 5d41402abc4b2a76b9719d911017c592
md5: 7μs
sha1: aaf4c61ddcc5e8a2dabede0f3b482cd9aea9434d
sha1: 7μs
sha256: 2cf24dba5fb0a30e26e83b2ac5b9e29e1b161e5c1fa7425e73043362938b9824
sha256: 8μs
sha512: 9b71d224bd62f3785d96d46ad3ea3d73319bfbc2890caadae2dff72519673ca723
23c3d99ba5c11d7c7acc6e14b8c5da0c4663475c2e5c3adef46f73bcdec043
sha512: 8μs
bcrypt: $2a$12$N.xKbRQZ10Bzd9QAFBFfBu2abQMUWZHsKcoctu30nU2iw2YI0DNwG
bcrypt: 283ms
scrypt: 736372797074001000000008000000005a539df65707e021f8afde283021dac7423
b8ebc3ecd5653b1dc0eb0a7e96c1212d95502588785cde34e05913cc874f9f496a2e388b83
994a3321413c15278915923dcf94b771d69cf64b53bc96282a28
scrypt: 640ms
```

As you can see, bcrypt takes about 0.3s to calculate and scrypt about 0.6s, whereas the rest are in microseconds. When cracking passwords this difference will translate every second into a timescale of days. That makes a huge difference when cracking passwords, since something that would otherwise take a day would now take more than 100 years.

bcrypt and scrypt also incorporate a salt to resist rainbow table attacks and are adaptive functions. This means that you can increase the calculation costs by changing the settings—making it resistive to brute force even when computational power increases dramatically.

I personally use bcrypt because it's easier to use than scrypt and my security requirements are usually not that high.

So how do you use it? Let's look at an example of a basic Mongoose model that uses bcrypt and hooks to store the password securely:

chp-7-authentication/mongoose-bcrypt.js
```js
'use strict';

var mongoose = require('mongoose');
var bcrypt = require('bcrypt');
var Schema = mongoose.Schema;

var accountSchema = new Schema({
    email:  { type: String, required: true, index: { unique: true } },
    password: { type: String, required: true }
});

// Define pre-save hook
```

```
accountSchema.pre('save', function (next) {
    var user = this;

    // only hash the password if it has been modified (or is new)
    if (!user.isModified('password')) {
        return next();
    }

    bcrypt.hash(user.password, 12, function (err, hash) {
        if(err) {
            next(err);
            return;
        }
        user.password = hash;
        next();
    });
});

// Define a method to verify password validity
accountSchema.methods.isValidPassword = function (password, callback) {

    bcrypt.compare(password, this.password, function (err, isValid) {
        if(err) {
            callback(err);
            return;
        }
        callback(null, isValid);
    });
};

module.exports = accountSchema;
```

With these tools, you can now store your user passwords in a manner that will keep attackers cracking at them for years.

## Enforce Password Strength Rules on Your Users

Now that we've covered storage, let's talk about the password itself. Most users aren't security conscious, so you have to help the user when selecting a password. The table on page 92 is a top-ten list of the most popular passwords from 2014[7] It's obvious that people don't really think about account security.

Don't let your users use common dictionary passwords, because your high-tech security measures are useless if the user is using monkey (position 12) or letmein (position 13) as a password. When the user selects a password, compare

---

7.   https://www.teamsid.com/worst-passwords-of-2014/.

| Position | Password | 2014 Rank | | Position | Password | 2014 Rank |
|----------|----------|-----------|---|----------|----------|-----------|
| 1. | 123456 | Unchanged | \| | 6. | 123456789 | Unchanged |
| 2. | password | Unchanged | \| | 7. | 1234 | Up 9 |
| 3. | 12345 | Up 17 | \| | 8. | baseball | New |
| 4. | 12345678 | Down 1 | \| | 9 | dragon | New |
| 5. | qwerty | Down 1 | \| | 10. | football | New |

Table 1—Top-ten Passwords of 2014

the string against a known dictionary of common passwords to make sure it isn't weak. You can easily find lists of common passwords[8] with a simple online search. The following example uses one such list to validate if the selected password exists in a dictionary:

```
chp-7-authentication/dictionary-validator.js
'use strict';

var fs = require('fs');

var dictionary = {};

// Since we are doing it only once on startup then use sync function
fs.readFileSync(__dirname + '/data/dictionary.txt', 'utf8')
    .split('\n')
    .forEach(function (password) {
        dictionary[password] = true;
    });

// This function will return an error message if the password is not good
// or false if it is proper
module.exports.isImproper = function check(username, password) {

    // About 3 percent of users derive the password from the username
    // This is not very secure and should be disallowed
    if(password.indexOf(username) !== -1) {
        return 'Password must not contain the username';
    }

    // Compare against dictionary
    if(dictionary[password]) {
        return 'Do not use a common password like: ' + password;
    }
    return false;
};
```

---

8. https://wiki.skullsecurity.org/index.php?title=Passwords

The more complete the dictionary, the better protection against weak passwords it will provide, but even the smallest dictionaries with just 500 common passwords would provide some protection.

To further increase password security, you should force the user to select stronger passwords. Instead of forcing the user to create passwords with special characters that are hard to remember, have them select longer passwords. Long passwords are easier to remember and offer better security because the resulting hashes take a longer time to crack.

Depending on the nature of the application, I also suggest the user should be forced to change passwords periodically, whether that's once a month, once a quarter, or even twice a year. This limits the timeframe in which attackers can try to break in with stolen passwords. And they have to start over and recrack the new password after every change. If you do require users to change their passwords, don't let them use previously used passwords. Just keep the previous hashes and compare the hash of the new one to make sure the user isn't trying to reuse the password.

Force users to use longer passwords, disallow common passwords, and change them periodically. These three tips will help keep data stored by your application safe.

## Move the Password Securely to the Server

We've established that the user needs to set a strong password and have covered how to store it. How do you move it from the web browser to the server? The first step, of course, is to use HTTPS. In fact, you should use HTTPS not just on login and registration pages but for the whole site. You will need HTTPS for login and registration pages to prevent man-in-the-middle attacks that try to steal passwords, but if you don't use HTTPS for the whole site, your session can still be stolen. This is discussed in length in Chapter 8, *Focus on Session Management*, on page 99.

Second, *do not send a plain-text password to the user's email* as a reminder. If the application is generating the password on the user's behalf, then force the user to change it immediately the first time the user logs in. Having a permanent plain-text record of a user's password in an email inbox is like the employee who writes passwords on Post-It notes and puts them next to the screen.

Third, *insert delays* in your login mechanism. We already covered brute-forcing at the storage level, but you can also slow down brute-forcing attempts on the application layer. A common way to do this is to punish the user for repeatedly failing to log into the application. You can ban the user for a while, such as fifteen minutes after five failed attempts, or make the user fill out a CAPTCHA challenge. Banning the user is a double-edged sword, because an attacker can maliciously block legitimate users by intentionally entering bad passwords, so use it carefully. The other approach is to create a universal delay for each failed login for a certain period of time. The legitimate user won't feel the delay; the attacker will.

Let's look at how you can ban the user's IP for a period of time if the user fails to log in a certain number of times:

```
chp-7-authentication/ban-user.js
var maxFailedCount = 5; // Max tries
var forgetFailedMins = 15; // time the user will be blocked
var blockList = {};

// Check if ip is still allowed
function isAllowed(ip) {
    return !blockList[ip] || blockList[ip].count < maxFailedCount;
}
// Remove ip from blockList
function successfulAttempt(ip) {
    if(blockList[ip]) {
        if(blockList[ip].timeout) {
            clearTimeout(blockList[ip].timeout);
        }
        delete blockList[ip];
    }
}
// Increment blocklist counter
function failedAttempt(ip) {
    if(!blockList[ip]) {
        blockList[ip] = {
            count: 0
        };
    }
    blockList[ip].count++;
    if(blockList[ip].timeout) {
        clearTimeout(blockList[ip].timeout);
    }
    blockList[ip].timeout = setTimeout(function () {
        delete blockList[ip];
    }, forgetFailedMins * 60 * 1000);
}

app.post('/login', function (req, res, next) {
    if(!isAllowed(req.ip)) { // Check if user is blocked
        req.session.error = 'You have been blocked for ' +
            forgetFailedMins + ' minutes';
```

```
        res.redirect('/');
        return;
    }
    validateUser(req.body, function(err, valid) {
        if(err) {
            next(err);
            return;
        }
        if(valid.success) { // Validation success. Create authorized session.
            successfulAttempt(req.ip); // Clear from blocklist
            req.session.login({userId: valid.userId}, function () {
                res.redirect('/user/' + valid.userId);
            });
        } else {
            failedAttempt(req.ip); // Register the failed attempt
            req.session.error = valid.error;
            res.redirect('/');
        }
    });
});
```

Node.js also lets us easily set a universal delay in answering:

chp-7-authentication/delay.js
```
app.post('/login', function (req, res, next) {
    function end(url) {
        setTimeout(function () {
            res.redirect(url);
        }, 1000);
    }
    validateUser(req.body, function(err, valid) {
        if(err) {
            next(err);
            return;
        }
        if(valid.success) { // Validation success. Create authorized session.
            req.session.login({userId: valid.userId}, function () {
                // delay before answer
                end('/user/' + valid.userId);
            });
        } else {
            req.session.error = valid.error;
            // delay before answering
            end('/');
        }
    });
});
```

However, the delay mechanism won't stop attackers from running parallel checks about a user's account. We can fix that problem, though:

```
chp-7-authentication/delay-no-parallel.js
// Map our authentications
var inProgress = {};

app.post('/login', function (req, res, next) {
    var key = req.ip + ':' + req.body.username;
    // check if we are already authenticating this user from the given IP
    if(inProgress[key]) {
        req.session.error = 'Authentication already in progress';
        res.redirect('/');
        return;
    }
    inProgress[key] = true;
    function end(url) {
        setTimeout(function () {
            delete inProgress[key];
            res.redirect(url);
        }, 1000);
    }
    validateUser(req.body, function(err, valid) {
        if(err) {
            delete inProgress[key];
            next(err);
            return;
        }
        if(valid.success) { // Validation success. Create authorized session.
            req.session.login({userId: valid.userId}, function () {
                // delay before answer
                end('/user/' + valid.userId);
            });
        } else {
            req.session.error = valid.error;
            // delay before answering
            end('/');
        }
    });
});
```

---

**Examples Are Not Production-Ready Code**

 The previous examples have been simplified and are not directly
usable in a production environment. For example, using session
to transfer the error message can cause issues. Holding the list
of in-progress validations in memory won't be valid if the process
is forked.

This will stop brute-force and dictionary attacks directly against the application
since the delays would slow down the attacker too much to make it worthwhile,
unless of course the user's password is in the top ten.

# Deal with the Fact That Users Will Forget

Humans are not computers and will forget things, even important things like credentials to an awesome web application such as yours. So let's talk about setting up a secure password-recovery mechanism.

The most common recovery system in modern web applications uses email. A link is sent to the registered email address to prompt the user to change the current (forgotten) password to a new one. While sufficient for most applications, if your application is extremely critical, you need a more secure recovery process. One option is to add a set of recovery questions or a secondary password that the user has to provide as part of the recovery process. This will stop attackers who have access of the victim's email inbox because they won't know the answers to those questions or the secondary password.

You should consider recovery answers as passwords that are intended to be easier to remember. As such they should also be hashed, and the application should validate the recovery questions as a group. If there are three questions, the person has to get the answers to all of them correct in order to proceed. If one of them is wrong, the person will be shown an error message, but this is important: do not specify which question was incorrect. The illustration shows the bad way to handle recovery questions (on the left) and the good way (on the right).

This is also how you would want to handle the actual login form. Do not say specifically if the username or the password was incorrect—just say that the combination was wrong. And as with login forms you also want to protect against brute-force attempts to figure out answers to recovery questions, so limit the number of attempts and insert delays.

With email-based recovery systems, always validate the user's email address, and don't let the user change it without revalidating it and using another layer of authentication. Without secondary verification when changing email addresses, an attacker who manages to break into the account can change the address unchallenged and permanently lock out the legitimate user.

## Add Other Authentication Layers for Better Security

For important applications, add another layer of authentication besides username and passwords. This will increase security because the attacker now has more layers to cut through. Some ways to achieve this include using hidden usernames, second passwords, and multi-factor authentication.

A hidden username is a two-username system. One is the username other users see and the other is used only for logging in. This is common in forums, where everyone sees a username, but you log in with your email address.

You can also let the user set up two passwords. The first password is used for logging in, and the second one is reserved for special requests and operations. One example is to use the second password to change the email address associated with the account. The session lifetime of the second password should be short. This will stop attackers who have gained access to the session or the first password from doing much damage.

Multi-factor authentication is becoming increasingly popular. The most common form, two-factor authentication, uses a third-party system like Google Authenticator to generate special codes. The idea is to force the user to log in with something only the user knows (a password) and something the user has (a phone running the Google Authenticator app, for example). This requires the attacker to also steal or compromise the phone in order to successfully log in. Multi-factor authentication schemes make credential theft much more difficult because the attacker has to bypass a second system to gain access.

## Wrapping Up

In this chapter we looked into hardening one of the backbones of web application security—authenticating the user. We looked at ways to store passwords securely, how to force users to use stronger passwords, how to protect against brute-force attacks, and how to add a second layer of protection.

Having covered the bases for authenticating a user, we now look at how the application remembers the user for a set period of time. We'll cover sessions in the next chapter so that your users won't have to keep typing in their password everytime they want to do something.

*Memory is the treasure house of the mind wherein the
monuments thereof are kept and preserved.*

➤ *Thomas Fuller*

# CHAPTER 8

# Focus on Session Management

In the last chapter we looked at authentication and how to make it difficult
for impersonators to steal credentials. This is critical for security, but we'd
lose users immediately if they were forced to retype their password every time
the application tried to do something. This is why we need sessions.

Think of sessions as pieces of your server's short-term memory. When you
authenticate to the application, the server remembers who you are for a set
amount of time. Sessions make the application convenient to use and your
users happy, but if you don't create and manage sessions securely, they'll
also make attackers happy. Sessions let attackers bypass the authentication
scheme, and there are multiple attack methods designed specifically to steal
user sessions. We look at some of the common attack and defense methods
in this chapter.

We'll start by setting up a session and then go through the implementation
of the more important guidelines to managing sessions in an application. For
a more thorough overview of what's important when managing sessions I
recommend reading the OWASP Session Management Cheat Sheet.[1]

## Set Up Sessions for Your Application

You can create sessions with query parameters, cookies, and tokens, to name
just a handful of ways. We'll start with the cookie-token-based sessions since
they're most commonly used.

Cookie-token sessions work by storing a token, also known as the sessionID,
in the cookie. The application regularly uses the token to look up session
information on the server side. Cookies are the preferred method for storing

---

1.  https://www.owasp.org/index.php/Session_Management_Cheat_Sheet

sessionIDs because they offer some control over the token's lifespan. They're also much more secure than using sessions based on the URL path.

Let's set up a session using the express framework. Since the middleware uses cookies to store the sessionID, we need to use the cookieParser middleware before the session middleware:

```
chp-8-session/express-memory-session.js
'use strict';

var express = require('express');
var session = require('express-session');
var cookieParser = require('cookie-parser');
var app = express();

app.use(cookieParser());
app.use(session({
    secret: 'this is a nice secret',
    resave: false,
    saveUninitialized: true
}));

app.get('/', function(req, res){
    if(!req.session.views) {
        req.session.views = 0;
    }
    req.session.views++;

    res.send('hello world. ' + req.session.views + ' times so far.');
});

app.listen(3000);
```

And that's it—we've set up a basic session. But we're far from finished.

The express-session default storage is a *MemoryStore*—a session implementation storing data in memory. This is not scalable, because it requires the web application to run as a single process and it also leaks memory. To mitigate this we need a different persistence layer.

In the following examples we'll use connect-redis,[2] which is a SessionStore implementation for the Redis[3] database. Redis is an excellent fit for session storage, since it's a fast key-value database, where keys can contain strings, hashes, lists, sets, and sorted sets.

---

2. https://github.com/visionmedia/connect-redis
3. http://redis.io/

To use Redis for the session storage we must install the Redis server, configure the SessionStore used by express, and set up a password for the database:

```
var express = require('express');
var RedisStore = require('connect-redis')(express); // Require connect-redis
var session = require('express-session');
var cookieParser = require('cookie-parser');
var app = express();

app.use(cookieParser());
app.use(session({
    store: new RedisStore({
        host: 'localhost',
        port: 6379,
        db: 2,
        pass: 'funky password here' // <- specify password
    }),
    secret: 'this is a nice secret',
    resave: false,
    saveUninitialized: true
}));
```

And that's it—we're now using Redis as our session storage. This allows us to scale horizontally because the database can be accessed by multiple processes from various machines simultaneously.

We could also use other storage systems like connect-mongo[4] or connect-sqlite3[5] or others, but we'll stick with Redis for our examples.

Although we now have session management, it's not secure, so let's look at how we can improve session security.

## Anonymize the sessionID Used

The first step for an attacker targeting a system is reconnaissance. The attacker researches the environment and narrows possible attack vectors to optimize the attack. As the defender, we want them to waste as much time as possible, so keeping the intruder guessing is a good move.

The default implementation of session in express and connect uses connect.sid as the sessionID token in the cookie. It's not hard to understand what technologies are in use based on that. To make it harder for possible attackers to gain information about the application's underlying systems, we need to use a more generic name for the sessionID:

---

4.   https://github.com/kcbanner/connect-mongo
5.   https://github.com/rawberg/connect-sqlite3

```
app.use(express.session({
    store: new RedisStore({
        host: 'localhost',
        port: 6379,
        db: 2,
        pass: 'funky password here'
    }),
    name: 'id', // <-- a generic name for the session id
    secret: 'this is a nice secret',
    resave: false,
    saveUninitialized: true
}));
```

With this configuration option, we can stop declaring to the world our session-handling mechanism and force the attacker to spend more time using various different attacks that don't impact our setup.

## Let the Session Die, aka Set a Time-to-Live

The MemoryStore session by default has no termination date—meaning if a user is signed in, then in theory, the user remains signed in forever. Since the default cookie expiration is undefined, *forever* in this case means as long as the browser is open. Without expiration information, the cookie gets deleted only if the browser closes.

The RedisStore implementation has a default Time-to-Live (TTL) of one day, which is a lot better but still not good enough. If you log into some website, say your bank, and move away from the computer, then it's bad if an hour later someone else can come along and still access your account. The OWASP recommendation is that session timeout be no longer than five minutes for highly protected applications and no more than twenty minutes for low-risk applications.

We can easily add a twenty-minute TTL to the application:

```
app.use(express.session({
    store: new RedisStore({
        host: 'localhost',
        port: 6379,
        db: 2,
        pass: 'funky password here',
        ttl: (20 * 60) // TTL of 20 minutes represented in seconds
    }),
    key: 'id', // use a generic id
    secret: 'this is a nice secret',
    resave: false,
    saveUninitialized: true
}));
```

Before you rush to implement a TTL, consider the application's content when selecting the timeout period. Sometimes you need more than twenty minutes. If the app has long, time-consuming forms or pages with lengthy text, then a longer timeout is necessary, or you should consider using a two-tier session system. It would be annoying if your email client threw you out every twenty minutes, wouldn't it?

A two-tier system is a session with two states: one for a short period immediately after logging in and the other that keeps you signed in but with a lower access level. Users can access less-secure areas for a longer period of time, but when trying to access more privileged areas, the user must authenticate again. A new session is created with privileged access for a short period of time and then degrades a to low-level session again. GitHub uses this mode, for example.

So how do you implement a two-tiered model? Let's extend the Session prototype with custom functions:

chp-8-session/express-redis-session-two-levels.js

```
var session = require('express-session');
var RedisStore = require('connect-redis')(session); // Require connect-redis

// Extend the Session prototype with some custom functions
// Add a login function
session.Session.prototype.login = function login() {
    // Set a time of login
    this.session._loggedInAt = Date.now();
};
// Add a function to check the logged in status of the user
session.Session.prototype.isLoggedIn = function isLoggedIn() {
    return !!this._loggedInAt;
};
// Add a function to check the freshness of the session
session.Session.prototype.isFresh = function isFresh() {
    // Return true if logged in less then 3 minutes ago
    return (this._loggedInAt && (Date.now() - this._loggedInAt) < (1000 * 60 * 3));
};
```

We can now use these functions in our application. We can check if the session is valid and allow privileged access if the session was validated recently.

chp-8-session/express-redis-session-two-levels.js

```
app.get('/', function(req, res){
    if(!req.session.views) {
        req.session.views = 0;
    }
    req.session.views++;
```

```
    res.send('hello world. ' + req.session.views + ' times so far.');
});

app.get('/login', function (req, res) {
    req.session.login()
    res.send('ok - ' + req.session._loggedInAt);
});


app.get('/secure', function (req, res) {
    if(!req.session.isLoggedIn()) { // Check if user is logged in
        res.send(401);
        return;
    }
    res.send('Access');
});

app.get('/secure/more', function (req, res) {
    if(!req.session.isFresh()) { // Check if session is fresh
        res.send(401);
        return;
    }
    res.send('You are fresh');
});

app.get('/logout', function (req, res) {
    req.session.destroy(); // Delete session
    res.redirect('/');
});
```

Now we're keeping the user logged in for longer periods of time for convenience without compromising security. Awesome, isn't it?

## Secure the Cookies so No One Can Steal Them

When you use cookies as a session identifier, you also need secure cookie handling. Attackers will try to steal cookies—or more specifically, the session token information stored in those cookies. This attack is called session hijacking because it relies on stealing the token to access the victim's authenticated session.

You have to first configure the server to limit your exposure and mitigate attack vectors like man-in-the-middle (MITM) and cross-site scripting (XSS). We've talked about MITM before in Chapter 3, *Start Connecting*, on page 23 and will cover XSS more thoroughly in Chapter 11, *Fight Cross-Site Scripts*, on page 139. To prevent MITM session hijacking attacks, you need to use HTTPS over the whole site and not just for login and registration pages. If you set up HTTPS, then also set the cookie as *secure*. This will stop the cookie from being sent unless it's part of an HTTPS request. It prevents situations where insecure content from the same domain is sent over HTTP along with the sessionID.

We can mitigate XSS attack vectors by preventing JavaScript from accessing the cookie contents. Use the httpOnly setting, which was specifically designed for that purpose, so that only browser requests have access to the cookie. Besides httpOnly, you can also limit the cookie's exposure by setting a minimum domain restriction. For example, if an *example.com* website has a well-defined logged-in section under the subdomain *secure.example.com*, there's no reason to send a cookie for every *\*.example.com* request. The more places you send your cookie, the larger your attack surface. So let's limit the cookie exposure to its minimum. The following example looks at how you prevent anyone from accessing the cookie:

```
app.use(express.session({
    store: new RedisStore({
        host: 'localhost',
        port: 6379,
        db: 2,
        pass: 'funky password here',
        ttl: (20 * 60)
    }),
    key: 'id',
    secret: 'this is a nice secret',
    resave: false,
    saveUninitialized: true
    cookie: {
        domain: 'secure.example.com' // limit the cookie exposure
        secure: true, // set the cookie only to be served with HTTPS
        path: '/',
        httpOnly: true, // Mitigate XSS
        maxAge: null
    }
}));
```

If possible, the path should also be set, but that means the user is always under a determined path after login. That's not a common scenario.

These configuration settings mitigate attacks against active sessions, but it might be possible to access the exchanged sensitive information from the browser's cache even after the session has been closed. This is especially relevant when considering public access points.

To improve the security of the application, the more sensitive parts of the website should not be cached. And at the very least, the sessionID should never be cached. The Cache-control header should be set to at least Cache-Control: no-cache="Set-Cookie, Set-Cookie2". You can do this using middleware:

```
// Set cache control header to eliminate cookies from cache
app.use(function (req, res, next) {
    res.header('Cache-Control', 'no-cache="Set-Cookie, Set-Cookie2"');
    next();
});
```

This will tell the browser not to save this information so it can't be accessed afterward.

## Re-create the Session When the User Logs In

Many web applications create a session even when the user isn't authenticated to track the user for marketing or other related reasons. These applications often make the mistake of escalating a non-authenticated session to an authenticated session by setting flags on the Session object. This isn't a secure approach because it leaves open the possibility for session-fixation attacks.

In session-fixation attacks, the attackers set the target's sessionID, and once the session is authenticated, they use that knowledge to hijack the session. This is why you should regenerate the sessionID every time session privileges are escalated.

You can do that by extending the express Session object's login function from the previous examples:

```
session.Session.prototype.login = function login(cb) {
    var req = this.req;
    this.regenerate(function (err) {
        if(err) {
            cb(err);
            return;
        }
        req.session._loggedInAt = Date.now();
        cb();
    });
};
```

Now we have an async login function on the Session object, so we have to redefine the login path:

```
app.get('/login', function (req, res) {
    req.session.login(function(err) {
        res.send('ok - ' + req.session._loggedInAt);
    });
});
```

The sessionID is now regenerated upon login, which mitigates the session-fixation attack vector. One more step toward secure sessions!

## Bind the Session to Prevent Hijacking

You can also take extra measures to avoid session hijacking attacks by binding the session to various user information such as the IP address or user agent. Since the information typically doesn't change mid-use, you can use it as a way to check if the session or account has been hijacked. If the information has changed, you know the session has a high probability of being hijacked and can take appropriate steps, including destroying the session, notifying the user, and logging for further analysis.

An experienced attacker can proxy the request through the same subnet to appear as the same IP address as the victim or change the user-agent information. Binding doesn't offer absolute protection, but it does place another hurdle for attackers to jump over.

Here, the previously defined login function is extended to bind the session variables:

chp-8-session/express-redis-session.js
```
session.Session.prototype.login = function login(cb) {
    var req = this.req;
    this.regenerate(function (err) {
        if(err) {
            cb(err);
            return;
        }
        req.session._loggedInAt = Date.now();
        req.session._ip = req.ip;
        req.session._ua = req.headers['user-agent'];
        cb();
    });
};
```

And here is the middleware to check the bindings. This middleware will check both the IP address and user agent against stored information in the session, and if the information deviates, then the whole session is thrown out:

chp-8-session/express-redis-session.js
```
// Check Session information
app.use(function (req, res, next) {

    if(!req.session) { // If there is no session then something is wrong
        next(new Error('Session object missing'));
        return;
    }
```

```
if(req.session.isGuest()) { // If not logged in then continue
    next();
    return;
}

if(req.session._ip !== req.ip) { // Check ip match
    // It would be wise to log more information here
    // to either notify the user or
    // to try and prevent further attacks
    console.warn('The request IP did not match session IP');

    // Generate a new unauthenticated session
    req.session.regenerate(function () {
        next();
    });
    return;
}

if(req.session._ua !== req.headers['user-agent']) { // Check UA validity
    // It would be wise to log more information here
    // to either notify the user or
    // to try and prevent further attacks
    console.warn('The request User Agent did not match session user agent');

    // Generate a new unauthenticated session
    req.session.regenerate(function () {
        next();
    });
    return;
}
// Everything checks out so continue
next();
});
```

The examples only address session hijacking, but you can use bindings to
also protect accounts from being hijacked. Instead of checking the session,
you store a list of expected IP addresses and user-agent values in the database.
If the user ever logs in with an unknown device or from an unknown location,
you can either notify the user about a suspicious login or ask for additional
verification. Some applications handle this by sending an email with a confir-
mation link.

There are caveats to binding the session to an IP address: if the user is using
a mobile device and moving around, for example, then the IP address changes
frequently. That would make binding inconvenient for the user, so keep that
in mind.

## Introducing the easy-session Module

I packaged most of the discussed session security functionality into a node module called easy-session[a] in order to make session regeneration, IP/UA checks, and two-level sessions easier to adopt.

Look at how easy it is to use it:

```
chp-8-session/express-redis-easy-session.js
var easySession = require('easy-session');
// Initialize easy session,
// with all the optional options
app.use(easySession.main(session, {
    ipCheck: true,
    uaCheck: true,
    freshTimeout: 5 * 60 * 1000,
    maxFreshTimeout: 10 * 60 * 1000
}));
```

This allows you to use simple functions to adopt the discussed protective methods:

```
chp-8-session/express-redis-easy-session.js
app.get('/', function(req, res){
    if(!req.session.views) {
        req.session.views = 0;
    }
    req.session.views++;

    res.send('hello world. ' + req.session.views + ' times so far.');
});

app.get('/login', function (req, res) {
    req.session.login(function(err) {
        res.send('ok - ' + req.session._loggedInAt);
    });
});

app.get('/logout', function (req, res) {
    req.session.logout(function (err) { // Logout
        res.redirect('/');
    });
});

app.get('/secure', easySession.isLoggedIn(), function (req, res, next) {
    res.send('secure');
});

app.get('/secure/more', easySession.isFresh(), function (req, res, next) {
    res.send('You are fresh');
});
```

---

a.      https://github.com/DeadAlready/node-easy-session

## Wrapping Up

In this chapter we looked at the session, an integral part of the authentication scheme. We started by setting up a session system and then added layers of security. We looked at how to add a Time-to-Live, secure cookies, mitigate session-fixation attacks, and add protections against hijacking.

We've covered our bases for authenticating a user and setting up a secure session, so in the next chapter we'll look at how to allow or deny user access to resources based on the user's access level.

*The opportunity to secure ourselves against defeat lies in our own hands, but the opportunity of defeating the enemy is provided by the enemy himself.*

➤ *Sun Tzu*

CHAPTER 9

# Set Up Access Control

In the previous chapters we set up authentication and sessions. We now know who is logged in and who is not. That's not enough; you don't want me to be able to see your information just because I'm logged into the same application. We need to be more specific, and for that we have to set up *access control*.

Access control defines and enforces the relationship between users and their privileges so that only the right users can access certain things in the application. In this chapter, we start with a refresher about the main access control methodologies and how they differ. While access control methods are generally simple to use, people make two common mistakes: missing *function-level access control* and insecure *direct object reference*. We'll also address how to avoid them in this chapter.

## Access Control Methods

The access control system's job is to figure out if a user should be allowed to run some function or see some data. There are different ways of distributing and then checking those rights; in this section we will discuss three of the most widely used methods in computer systems: *mandatory/discretionary access control* (MAC/DAC), *identity-based access control* (IBAC), and *role-based access control* (RBAC).

MAC and DAC are both focused on the data objects instead of the users. Upon authorization the user is assigned to a group, and the access decisions are based on the settings of the data object in question. The DAC model allows the owner of the data object to determine the access-level requirements at the owner's discretion—hence the name. This is a common model found in UNIX systems where the access rights to files and folders are determined by the owner. The MAC model is similar in the access decision making; however, the access-level requirements are not at the discretion of the owner but are instead mandatory based on the sensitivity of the data. The latter system is mainly only used in systems with high security requirements because it's difficult to implement.

IBAC is an access control method that focuses on the identity of the user. It's usually implemented with an *access control list (ACL)*—a list of users that specifies what operations each person has access to. It's granular and simple, making it a good approach for non-complex systems with a limited number of users. Remember the KISS (Keep it simple, stupid) methodology.

Represented as a table, an ACL might look something like this:

| User | Operation | | | |
|------|-----------|-------|--------|---------|
|      | Read | Write | Delete | Publish |
| Karl | ✓ | ✓ | ✓ | ✓ |
| Jill | ✓ | ✓ | ✓ | — |
| Jack | ✓ | ✓ | — | — |
| John | ✓ | — | — | — |

But an ACL table will be hard to maintain for a complex system with lots of users. If you develop a new feature, you'll have to go through the whole table and decide on a per-user basis whether to assign the rights for that user. This applies for every change you make to the system.

Imagine that this is just the beginning of a table with thousands of users and tens of different privileges, and you'll see how maintaining it can quickly become a problem:

| User | Operation | | | | | | | |
|------|------|-------|--------|---------|--------|--------|--------|--------|
|      | Read | Write | Delete | Publish | Create | Revoke | Upload | Change |
| Karl | ✓ | ✓ | ✓ | ✓ | ✓ | ✓ | ✓ | ✓ |
| Jill | ✓ | ✓ | ✓ | ✓ | ✓ | ✓ | ✓ | — |
| Jack | ✓ | — | — | — | — | — | — | — |
| John | ✓ | ✓ | ✓ | — | — | — | — | — |
| William | ✓ | — | — | — | — | — | — | — |
| Thomas | ✓ | ✓ | ✓ | ✓ | ✓ | ✓ | ✓ | — |
| Florence | ✓ | ✓ | ✓ | ✓ | — | — | — | — |
| Alice | ✓ | — | — | — | — | — | — | — |
| Logan | ✓ | — | — | — | — | — | — | — |
| Alexis | ✓ | ✓ | ✓ | — | — | — | — | — |
| Olivier | ✓ | ✓ | ✓ | ✓ | ✓ | ✓ | ✓ | — |
| Leah | ✓ | — | — | — | — | — | — | — |
| Emma | ✓ | — | — | — | — | — | — | — |
| Félix | ✓ | ✓ | ✓ | ✓ | — | — | — | — |
| Liam | ✓ | — | — | — | — | — | — | — |
| Olivia | ✓ | ✓ | ✓ | ✓ | ✓ | ✓ | ✓ | — |
| Nathan | ✓ | ✓ | ✓ | — | — | — | — | — |
| Jacob | ✓ | — | — | — | — | — | — | — |
| Zoé | ✓ | — | — | — | — | — | — | — |
| Rosalie | ✓ | ✓ | ✓ | — | — | — | — | — |

RBAC is an access control method that was designed to alleviate the problem of managing large ACL tables. It does this by consolidating rights into logical groups—roles. Now, instead of defining for each individual all the different access rights, you simply specify which role they belong to and the access rights are determined by the role. It's meant to mimic real-world access rights management.

This means our previous example would become two separate tables. One to determine the access rights of the roles:

| Role | Operation | | | | | | | |
|------|-----------|-------|--------|---------|--------|--------|--------|--------|
| | Read | Write | Delete | Publish | Create | Revoke | Upload | Change |
| Admin | ✓ | ✓ | ✓ | ✓ | ✓ | ✓ | ✓ | ✓ |
| Manager | ✓ | ✓ | ✓ | ✓ | ✓ | ✓ | ✓ | — |
| Publisher | ✓ | ✓ | ✓ | ✓ | — | — | — | — |
| Writer | ✓ | ✓ | ✓ | — | — | — | — | — |
| Reader | ✓ | — | — | — | — | — | — | — |

And one to determine the roles of individuals.

| User | Role | | User | Role | | User | Role | | User | Role |
|------|------|---|------|------|---|------|------|---|------|------|
| Karl | Admin | | Thomas | Manager | | Olivier | Admin | | Olivia | Manager |
| Jill | Manager | | Florence | Publisher | | Leah | Reader | | Nathan | Writer |
| Jack | Reader | | Alice | Reader | | Emma | Reader | | Jacob | Reader |
| John | Writer | | Logan | Reader | | Félix | Publisher | | Zoé | Reader |
| William | Reader | | Alexis | Writer | | Liam | Reader | | Rosalie | Writer |

We lose a little granularity, but it's already much simpler to manage, as you can see. Instead of having to manage all the individuals in case of new functionality, you just manage the associated roles. RBAC in web applications is also often implemented with inheritance logic to further simplify the assignment of rights. Let's look at an example.

Some system has the roles reader, writer, editor, and admin. The reader can read the posts, so that would be anyone coming to the application. The writer can read and write new posts, so this would be a few select people. The editor can modify the posts and then publish them. And the administrator can do everything. We can see all the roles in the following Venn diagram:

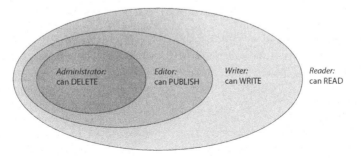

In this system we can see that each role inherits all the rights of the parent role and then adds some of its own. If you want to create a second type of internal post that everyone who isn't a reader can read and only administrators can write, then you just have to modify the rights associated with the appropriate roles (in this case writer and administrator):

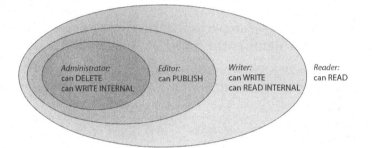

There are dozens of modules written for both ACL and RBAC in Node.js to help you implement proper access control for your application, such as acl[1] or easy-rbac.[2] The principles aren't complicated, and implementation is fairly straightforward. You just assign the rights to users and check if users have the correct privileges when needed. Yet people frequently make mistakes with access control. Let's review some common implementation issues. What's more common than forgetting to lock your door?

## Missing Function-Level Access Controls in Your Code

The most common mistake people make when implementing access control is misplacing or poorly implementing validation in the code. That means you don't have access control right before the action that requires it. In this situation, attackers can circumvent access control by figuring out how the application handles the access checks.

For example, path validation mismanagement occurs when private functionality is hidden from unauthorized users on the client side, but no corresponding check is performed on the server side. An attacker who knows the application well enough would be able to access restricted functionality.

This example consists of a web application that builds a menu based on the user's authentication status. Logged-out users see three links, whereas users with permission see four:

---

1.  https://www.npmjs.com/package/acl
2.  https://www.npmjs.com/package/easy-rbac

chp-9-access-control/client-side.js
```
// Function to build menu
function getNav(req, cb) {
    var html = '<nav>' +
        '<a href="/page/1">Page 1</a> ' +
        '<a href="/page/2">Page 2</a> ' +
        '<a href="/page/3">Page 3</a> ';

    req.session.can('read users', function (err, can){
        if(!err && can) {
            html += '<a href="/users">Users</a>';
        }
        cb(null, html);
    });
}


// Show a welcome message
app.get('/', function (req, res, next) {
    getNav(req, function (err, html) {
        res.send(html + '<br/><div>Welcome home</div>');
    });
});
```

Let's look at the functionality of the links:

chp-9-access-control/client-side.js
```
// Regular pages, show what page we are on
app.get('/page/:nr', function (req, res, next){
    getNav(req, function (err, html) {
        res.send(html + '<div>Page ' + req.params.nr +'</div>');
    });
});


// Our admin function to show users
app.get('/users', function (req, res, next) {
    getNav(req, function (err, html) {
        res.send(html + '<pre>' + JSON.stringify(db.users, '', 2) +'</pre>');
    });
});
```

/page paths show different pages, but for admin accounts there's also the /users path, which shows all the accounts of this website in JSON format. Do you see what's wrong with this picture?

The problem is that the only authentication is in the construction of client-side HTML. But if the attacker knows (has seen, mapped, or otherwise gathered information) that there's also the path /users meant for administrators, then the attacker can visit the path and see that part of the application. No authentication is required—only knowledge that it exists.

As you know by now, this isn't a secure scenario. So let's fix this by adding an access check to the function:

```
// Our admin function to show users
app.get('/users', function (req, res, next) {
    // Check access
    req.session.can('read users', function (err, can) {
        if(err || !can) {
            res.sendStatus(403); // Send forbidden
            return;
        }
        getNav(req, function (err, html) {
            res.send(html +
                '<pre>' + JSON.stringify(db.users, '', 2) +'</pre>');
        });
    });
});
```

Now the path /users will return as unauthorized. The authorization check is done immediately before the execution, eliminating this attack vector. Depending on the nature of the application and the function, you can also add a bit of obfuscation to the mix:

```
// Our admin function to show users
app.get('/users', function (req, res, next) {
    // Check access
    req.session.can('read users', function (err, hasAccess) {
        if(err || !can) {
            console.warn('Unauthorized access attempt', req.path, err);
            next(); // Move along
            return;
        }
        getNav(req, function (err, html) {
            res.send(html +
                '<pre>' + JSON.stringify(db.users, '', 2) +'</pre>');
        });
    });
});
```

By simply moving on to the next() function, you refuse to even acknowledge the existence of this function—this prevents attackers from learning (or confirming) that there's a privileged function at this path. At the same time, it can make development a hassle. Logging is added precisely for that reason—without it you get no feedback whatsoever as a developer. For a more thorough overview of why logging is important, you can review *Decide What Gets Logged*, on page 29.

## Pay Attention to Client-Side Forms

Paths aren't the only client-side problems you have to worry about. It's common for applications to validate forms on the client side, but that should never be the only data validation layer. *Client-side validation does not substitute for server-side validation.*

Security checks on the client side can be easily circumvented, such as by using a custom browser or proxy. Consider what happens if you have an application with a registration form and you're a logged-in user (or administrator) who can add other administrator users. Unauthorized users don't see this option on the form, but you do. The constructor would look something like the menu constructor you saw previously:

```
chp-9-access-control/client-side-form.js
// Show registration form
app.get('/register', function (req, res, next) {
    var form = '<form method="POST">' +
        '<input type="text" name="username" placeholder="username" />' +
        '<input type="text" name="name" placeholder="name" />' +
        '<input type="text" name="company" placeholder="company" />';

    // If has rights then show admin checkbox
    req.session.can('add admins', function (err, has) {
        if(!err && has) {
            form += '<label for="isAdmin">Is Admin? ' +
            '<input id="isAdmin" type="checkbox" name="isAdmin" value="1" />' +
            '</label>';
        }
        form += '<input type="submit" value="Submit" />' +
        '</form>';

        res.send(form);
    });

});
```

To complete the circle of bad access control, let's add a form handler:

```
chp-9-access-control/client-side-form.js
// Post request handler
app.post('/register', function (req, res, next){
    // Check username
    if(db.users[req.body.username]) {
        res.sendStatus(409);
        return;
    }

    var newUser = {
```

```
        name: req.body.name,
        company: req.body.company,
        isAdmin: req.body.isAdmin || 0 // if no isAdmin is sent then set to 0
    };
    db.users[req.body.username] = newUser;

    console.log(db.users); // show us the users
    res.redirect('/');
});
```

We should now see some users listed in db.users after completing the registration form a few times:

```
{
    'admin': { name: 'Admin', company: 'This', isAdmin: 1 },
    'karl': { name: 'karl', company: 'Karl', isAdmin: 0 }
}
```

But since no check is performed on the data that was posted, an unauthorized user could also send the isAdmin field using a cURL request to modify the data in db.users:

```
curl 'http://localhost:3000/register' \
-H 'Content-Type: application/x-www-form-urlencoded' \
--data 'username=attack&name=attack&company=attack&isAdmin=1'
```

New users can be added to db.users, which is now a problem:

```
{
    'admin': { name: 'Admin', company: 'This', isAdmin: 1 },
    'attack': { name: 'attack', company: 'attack', isAdmin: 1 }
}
```

I think you see where we're going with this. If you perform access checking right before the action, you prevent the unauthorized registrations:

```
// Post request handler
app.post('/register', function (req, res, next){

    // Check username
    if(db.users[req.body.username]) {
        res.sendStatus(409);
        return;
    }

    var newUser = {
        name: req.body.name,
        company: req.body.company,
        isAdmin: 0 // Default to false
    };
```

```
    // check if we are authorized to set the flag and set if allowed
    req.session.can('add admins', function (err, can) {
        if(!err && can) {
            newUser.isAdmin = req.body.isAdmin || 0;
        }

        db.users[req.body.username] = newUser;

        console.log(db.users); // show us the users
        res.redirect('/');
    });
});
```

Performing the access check right before the actual operation is the key to keeping the application secure.

## Don't Forget About Server-Side Validation

The most common server-side mistakes involve misconfigured access validation. It usually occurs when authentication is expected but it doesn't happen or is forgotten. Let's modify the last section's registration form by adding a whole separate path. The form will be the same for both /register and /add-admin, but the handling is different. First we set up the routes:

chp-9-access-control/server-side.js

```
// Show registration form
app.get('/register', function (req, res, next) {
    res.send(getForm());
});

// Post request handler for regular users
app.post('/register', function (req, res, next){
    addUser(req.body, false); // Add a regular user
    res.redirect('/');
});

// Authentication middleware
app.get('*', easySession.can('add admin'));

// Show the admin user adding form
app.get('/add-admin', function (req, res, next) {
    res.send(getForm('/add-admin'));
});

// Post request handler for adding admin users
app.post('/add-admin', function (req, res, next) {
    addUser(req.body, true); // Add admin user
    res.redirect('/');
});
```

When you visit the site you see only the /register link, which allows you to add a regular user. Even if you use the previous example's cURL request, only a regular user is added. Additionally, even if the attacker knows that there is an /add-admin path, visiting it will show an Unauthorized error message.

Even though everything seems secure, it really isn't.

Because we have misconfigured the authentication middleware, it doesn't apply to POST requests, only GET. An attacker only has to change the action of the form, the POST path. This would let non-logged-in users add adminstrator users:

```
curl 'http://localhost:3000/add-admin' \
-H 'Content-Type: application/x-www-form-urlencoded' \
--data 'username=attack&name=attack&company=attack&isAdmin=1'
```

First, let's fix the middleware registration to work for all requests, not just GET:

```
// Authentication middleware
app.all('*', easySession.can('add admin')); // all instead of get
```

You can also decide to use the middleware specifically before each route. The benefit of this approach is that you always see if authentication is there or not. The downside is that you'd have to write it every time:

```
// Show the admin user adding form
app.get('/add-admin', easySession.can('add admin'), function (req, res, next) {
    res.send(getForm('/add-admin'));
});

// Post request handler for adding admin users
app.post('/add-admin', easySession.can('add admin'), function (req, res, next) {
    addUser(req.body, true); // Add admin user
    res.redirect('/');
});
```

Always remember to do access validation, and always test the expected behavior to avoid mistakes associated with improperly placed validation. Don't forget to perform server-side validation no matter how much validation exists on the client side. And the best place to perform authentication and validation is directly before the executable function or at the beginning of the function itself. This way, attackers can't circumvent the authentication via some loophole.

# Don't Use Insecure Direct Object References

Applications often use names, identifiers, or keys of objects when generating web pages. Sometimes they forget to validate the user's access to a specific object. This becomes a problem after validation when an authenticated user can still access objects that aren't supposed to be accessible. And they can do it by knowing or guessing the keys of other objects.

This is similar to the missing path validation issues we discussed earlier, except this applies to dynamically generated pages. Let's look at an in-memory database, db, which stores the user data. Users can log in and see the data via the settings page on /settings/:id:

```
chp-9-access-control/idor.js
// Middleware to validate that users are authenticated
app.all('*', function (req, res, next) {
    if(req.session.isGuest()) {
        res.send(401);
        return;
    }
    next();
});

app.get('/settings/:id', easySession.isLoggedIn(), function (req, res) {
    res.json(db[req.params.id]);
});
```

For example, Johann will see the following when visiting /settings/1:

```
{
    "username": "johann",
    "password": "pw",
    "name": "Johann",
    "company": "Mixo",
    "role": "user",
    "age": 32
}
```

In this application the right to access this information is not authenticated, so after logging in, Johann could change the URL to /settings/2 (not too hard to guess) and see information about other users.

This is a common mistake—not validating if the user has access rights to a directly referenced object. This is a problem especially if the references are logically guessable or known.

So how do we fix this? There are two main mitigation techniques that you can use to solve an insecure direct object reference issue.

First, *do not use direct references unless they are necessary.* For example, the previous application should not use the userId from the request parameter but instead use the session userId. This removes the user's control over parameters.

```
app.get('/settings', function (req, res) {
    // Use session variable instead of a GET variable
    res.json(db[req.session.userId]);
});
```

This approach solves the problem by removing the underlying issue, but it's not always feasible. Sometimes, you just can't avoid direct references. For example, in the previous application, you might want to provide the administrator access to all accounts.

So let's take a different approach. Keep in mind the second rule: *validate access rights to an object when the object is accessed.* You need to validate the user and that person's right to access the current object at the point of access. We can fix the example by rewriting the route handler:

```
chp-9-access-control/idor-mitigation.js
app.get('/settings/:id*?', easySession.isLoggedIn(), function (req, res) {
    // If there is no GET parameter
    if(!req.params.id) {
        // Use session variable instead of a GET variable
        res.json(db[req.session.userId]);
        return;
    }
    // If we are accessing our own info or we are admin
    if(req.session.userId === +req.params.id ||
        db[req.session.userId].username === 'admin'){

        res.json(db[req.params.id]);
        return;
    }
    res.sendStatus(403); // forbidden
});
```

This route handler will by default serve the session user information. But you can still send a GET parameter with the requested userID if you need to. Either way, before you display the information, the application validates to make sure the user is allowed to see this information.

After logging in with Johann's account, you can request the user information from /settings or /settings/1; however, /settings/3 will return Forbidden. But if you log in with admin, then you can request any /settings/:id that exists and get the appropriate response.

This is part of deep authentication methodology, where authentication is woven into an application on every level and not just applied as a layer on top. It's also a definite requirement for good security and emphasizes how important it is to validate at the point of access.

However, the previous example also features one of the common anti-patterns of access control implementation—hardcoded role checks. Checking for various combinations of access modifiers using inline if statements is not scalable and is error prone should there be a need for change. So instead of the following code:

```
if(req.session.userId === +req.params.id ||
    db[req.session.userId].username === 'admin'){

    res.json(db[req.params.id]);
    return;
}
```

You should use something more generic such as:

```
var params = {
    userId: req.session.userId,
    id: +req.params.id
};
// Check access
req.session.can('access user', params, function (err, has) {
    if(err || !has) {
        res.sendStatus(403);
        return;
    }
    res.json(db[req.params.id]);
});
```

This way, if the access control has to be changed, it can be changed in the definition of the operation or the roles instead of having to go over all possible implementation points.

## Wrapping Up

Having users sign in to get access to advanced functionality isn't always enough. Access control lets you differentiate between users and enforce what they can access. In this chapter, we discussed the similarities and differences of various access control methods.

Then we moved on to discuss how access validation should always be done as close to the actual operation as possible. We also established that you should avoid direct object references to privileged objects where possible. And finally, we covered that you shouldn't just validate a user's access level but also validate access to specific objects.

We've set up our full application stack, but we're missing one vital component—functionality. In the next chapters we'll discuss how you can write functionality without making yourself an easy target for attackers—starting with denial of service in the next chapter.

*It does not matter how slowly you go*
*as long as you do not stop.*

➤ *Confucius*

CHAPTER 10

# Defend Against Denial-of-Service Attacks

In the previous chapter, we set up proper authentication and access control mechanisms for our web application. Now it's time to add features and flesh out our application, but we want to do it securely. We don't want to be the proverbial baby holding candy for the attackers.

In this chapter we examine one of the more common and simple attack methods that exists in the wild today: *denial-of-service attacks*. Let's go over what exactly constitutes a DoS attack, and then you'll learn how to identify and avoid anti-patterns such as asymmetry, synchronous code, and poor memory management. By the end of this chapter you should be able to avoid mistakes that would allow an easy or even accidental DoS attack against your Node.js application.

---

**No Cluster in this Chapter**

 In the following sections we ignore the fact that you can run a Node.js process as a cluster, as this only alleviates the problem by a constant factor (the number of processes). Since it isn't all that helpful, we'll keep it simple and stick with a single thread.

## Recognize Denial-of-Service Attacks

A denial-of-service (DoS) or distributed denial-of-service (DDoS) attack is an attempt to make a machine or network resource unavailable. The means to carry out, motives for, and targets of a DoS attack vary widely. In general, attacks consist of efforts to temporarily or indefinitely interrupt or suspend services. As the name implies, DDoS attacks are sent by more than one person or bot, while DoS attacks are typically the work of one person or system.

There may be many reasons for attackers to want your application to be unusable—perhaps they're competitors or just bored kids—but the bottom line is a DoS attack is bad for your business. It increases the running costs and messes with the availability of your service. It's clearly something you want to avoid.

The following is a screenshot of the current reported network state from an interactive DDoS monitoring site—the Digital Attack Map[1] from Arbor Networks. That's a lot of attacks on a given day.

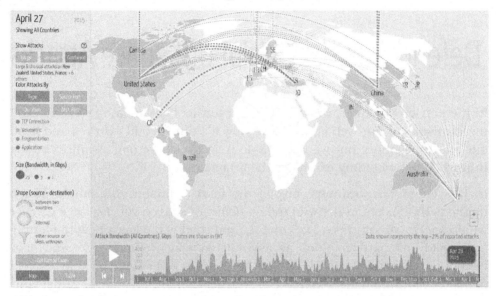

Attack methods vary, ranging from flooding the server's Internet connection to a point where it's no longer usable by legitimate users, to more complex methods targeting the application's configuration or routing. Other methods take advantage of limited resources, such as the number of concurrent connections allowed by Apache. Some attacks can even go after the physical network components.

Fortunately, Node.js is resilient to flooding attacks since there's no limit on the number of concurrent requests and the process is events based. *Slowloris* attacks, which exploit the limited number of concurrent requests, simply don't apply to Node.js applications. A flaw made earlier versions of Node.js vulnerable, but if you're using version 0.10.21 or newer, you won't be affected.

Obviously, the first line of defense is the server's firewall. While the firewall needs to be configured properly, doing so is not in the context of this book. Instead, we move on to look at synchronous code. Node.js programs and libraries try hard to avoid this problem, but it keeps crawling back in.

---

1.  http://www.digitalattackmap.com/

# Avoid Synchronous Code in Your Application

As you know, Node.js is built around events. The whole process is a big event machine juggling different flows. Since our main process is single threaded, any function that takes a while to execute should be done in an evented manner to avoid locking up the entire application.

If you're used to working in other programming languages, this is a tricky concept to get accustomed with. Let's look at an example, where we implement a recursive Fibonacci calculation and a server to allow access to it:

chp-10-dos/fibonacci.js

```javascript
'use strict';

var express = require('express');
var app = express();

// Calculating fibonacci number recursively
function fibonacci(n) {
    if(n < 3) {
        return 1;
    }
    return fibonacci(n - 1) + fibonacci(n - 2);
}

app.get('/:n*?', function (req, res) {
    if(!req.params.n) {
        res.send('Hello');
        return;
    }
    var fib = fibonacci(+req.params.n);
    res.send('Fibonacci nr ' + req.params.n + ' is ' + fib);
});

app.listen(3000);
```

Now the client can ask for a Fibonacci calculation by going to a path like /7 and get a result of Fibonacci nr 7 is 13.

Let's ignore that this is an inefficient way to calculate Fibonacci and focus on the fact that it's synchronous. If a user enters a large number, the whole process gets locked up in that one calculation, and no one else gets a response before this one finishes. To put things in context, it takes this method sixteen seconds to calculate the forty-sixth number on my machine. During those sixteen seconds, all other requests are simply hanging.

Yes, this is an artificial problem, but it illustrates why you should move intensive calculations or long operations into a separate process or split them into chunks that can run in an evented manner. We can fix our Fibonacci example by moving the calculation into a separate calculation file:

chp-10-dos/fibonacci-calc.js

```
// Calculating fibonacci number recursively
function fibonacci(n) {
    if(n < 3) {
        return 1;
    }
    return fibonacci(n - 1) + fibonacci(n - 2);
}

console.log(fibonacci(process.argv[2]));
```

We can then rewrite the application to invoke the process in the new file. It's not the most optimal way, but it clearly demonstrates how you can move long calculations into separate processes:

chp-10-dos/fibonacci-separate.js

```
'use strict';

var express = require('express');
var app = express();

var exec = require('child_process').exec;

app.get('/:n*?', function (req, res) {
    if(!req.params.n) {
        res.send('Hello');
        return;
    }

    // Execute the separate calculation file
    var cmd = 'node ' + __dirname + '/fibonacci-calc.js ' + parseInt(req.params.n);
    exec(cmd, function (err, stdout, stderr) {
        //FIXME: We should use execFile here
        //FIXME: We should handle possible errors here

        res.send('Fibonacci nr ' + req.params.n + ' is ' + parseInt(stdout));
    });

});

app.listen(3000);
```

Another solution is to use callbacks or EventEmitters to create events. Let's see how you can do Fibonacci using callbacks:

## Use the Right Tool for the Job

When creating separate process files or doing heavy calculations, it's not wise to always stick to Node.js. Starting a Node.js process takes a lot of resources and isn't always the most efficient way to solve problems. Instead, try to use optimal libraries suited for the task. In the end it's about choosing the right tool for the job.

chp-10-dos/fibonacci-callback-sync.js

```javascript
'use strict';

var express = require('express');
var app = express();

// Non blocking fibonacci recursive
function fibonacci(n, cb) {
    if(n < 3) {
        // return the number in the callback
        cb(1);
        return;
    }

    var sum = 0;
    function end(subN) {
        if(sum !== 0) {
            cb(sum + subN);
        } else {
            sum += subN;
        }
    }
    // Start calculation of previous two numbers
    fibonacci(n - 1, end);
    fibonacci(n - 2, end);
}

app.get('/:n*?', function (req, res) {
    if(!req.params.n) {
        res.send('Hello');
        return;
    }

    // Execute the separate calculation file
    fibonacci(+req.params.n, function (result) {
        res.send('Fibonacci nr ' + req.params.n + ' is ' + result);
    })

});

app.listen(3000);
```

Don't start celebrating the callbacks just yet. This calculation is still not asynchronous. Just because you're using a callback, it doesn't automatically make a function asynchronous. This is a common misassumption and frequently shows up in situations like the following example:

```
function someFn(input, callback) {
    if(input.hasError) {
        callback(new Error('Invalid input'));
        return;
    }
    // Do our stuff
}
```

While someFn() might be asynchronous most of the time, if you have an error in the input, the callback gets called synchronously. This can result in some strange behaviors for the application:

```
function useSomeFn(req, res) {
    // Start information query as soon as possible
    someFn({hasError:true}, function (err, data) {
        if(err) {
            res.send(500);
            return;
        }
        res.json(data);
    });
    // Set some cookies in the meantime
    res.cookie('my', 'cookie');
}
```

Let's assume someFn() is asynchronous and set some cookies. When the result comes back from the server, you can respond to the client. This is a good idea, but if the input has an error, then the callback is executed before the cookie setting, resulting in a headers already sent error. This is a hard thing to debug if you don't know what you're looking for.

In these situations, you can use setImmediate(). We can fix someFn() to work properly so that even the error message is sent asynchronously:

```
function someFn(input, callback) {
    if(input.hasError) {
        setImmediate(callback, new Error('Invalid input'));
        return;
    }
    // Do our stuff
}
```

Now let's use setImmediate() to also fix our Fibonacci function:

chp-10-dos/fibonacci-callback.js

```javascript
'use strict';

var express = require('express');
var app = express();

// Non blocking fibonacci recursive
// NOTE: it is slow
function fibonacci(n, cb) {
    if(n < 3) {
        // return the number in the callback
        // as resources allow
        setImmediate(cb, 1);
        return;
    }

    var sum = 0;
    function end(subN) {
        if(sum !== 0) {
            setImmediate(cb, sum + subN);
        } else {
            sum += subN;
        }
    }
    // Start calculation of previous two numbers
    setImmediate(fibonacci, n - 1, end);
    setImmediate(fibonacci, n - 2, end);
}

app.get('/:n*?', function (req, res) {
    if(!req.params.n) {
        res.send('Hello');
        return;
    }

    // Execute the separate calculation file
    fibonacci(+req.params.n, function (result) {
        res.send('Fibonacci nr ' + req.params.n + ' is ' + result);
    })

});

app.listen(3000);
```

The Fibonacci function is now asynchronous. However, creating functions on every iteration of a recursive function means we'll soon run out of memory.

While this Fibonacci calculation is somewhat artificial, these types of problems are fairly common. They occur when developers use synchronous file system functions such as fs.readFileSync(). These synchronous functions should be used rarely in web server code and are considered safe only during application startup. Synchronous code in Node.js is generally a bad thing and should be avoided while processing requests. This isn't a hard and fast rule—if you're writing a command-line utils library, synchronous code is not a bad thing. But then again, no one is going to try to DDoS your utils library, either.

Finding performance issues isn't always intuitive, especially if the application codebase is large. There are several tools you should consider using, such as Chrome DevTools plus Node Inspector,[2] Spy.js,[3] and Node WebKit Agent.[4]

You should now know why and how to avoid synchronous code in your application, but this isn't the only possible problem. As we saw with the last asynchronous version of the Fibonacci, memory can also be a problem, so we'll discuss memory management next.

## Manage How Your Application Uses Memory

Since the process thread is shared among all the clients, memory is also shared. You should avoid storing much information in memory per request because it can accumulate over concurrent clients and your process can die simply because it runs out of memory. In threaded servers, a thread usually has a separate memory limit that's reached long before the whole server process runs out of memory, so only the thread gets terminated instead of the whole process. However, Node.js, being in a single thread, will kill the whole process. Let's look at a common mistake where memory is overtaxed:

chp-10-dos/memory/memory-error.js
```
'use strict';

var express = require('express');
var app = express();

var fs = require('fs');

app.get('/getfile', function (req, res) {
    fs.readFile(__dirname + '/dictionary.txt', 'utf8', function (err, content) {
        res.send(err ? 500 : content); // send an error or content of file
    });
});

app.listen(3000);
```

---

2. https://github.com/node-inspector/node-inspector
3. http://spy-js.com
4. https://github.com/c4milo/node-webkit-agent

It looks perfectly fine, doesn't it? When the client requests a file, the application reads it from the file system (asynchronously, as it should) and then sends it to the client. The problem is that the whole file is read into memory before it's sent to the client. In our example, the file is small, so it doesn't really matter. But if the file was larger—a few hundred MB, for example—then it could create a memory issue.

How do you fix this? Streams.

A basic building block in Node.js and a type of EventEmitter, streams are widely used. Streams allow us to transmit the file to the client application bit by bit as it becomes available so that we don't hog memory no matter how big the file. Let's look at how to fix the previous example with streams:

chp-10-dos/memory/memory-stream.js
```
'use strict';

var express = require('express');
var app = express();

var fs = require('fs');

app.get('/getfile', function (req, res) {
    fs.createReadStream(__dirname + '/dictionary.txt', 'utf8').pipe(res);
});

app.listen(3000);
```

Or in this case we could use express framework's res.sendFile for more consistent file handling:

chp-10-dos/memory/memory-sendfile.js
```
app.get('/getfile', function (req, res) {
    res.sendFile(__dirname + '/dictionary.txt', 'utf8');
});
```

While there are cases when you need the whole file before you can perform some kind of operation, in most situations you can work with the file a little at a time, for example, when sending the hash of the file:

chp-10-dos/memory/memory-hash.js
```
'use strict';

var express = require('express');
var app = express();

var fs = require('fs');
var crypto = require('crypto');
```

```
app.get('/getfile', function (req, res) {
    var stream = fs.createReadStream(__dirname + '/dictionary.txt', 'utf8');
    var hash = crypto.createHash('md5');

    //FIXME: Add error handling
    stream.on('data', function (data) {
        hash.update(data);
    });

    stream.on('end', function () {
        res.send(hash.digest('hex'));
    });
});

app.listen(3000);
```

With Node.js, you can keep the memory footprint small when making requests. Do things bit by bit, and don't load huge amounts of data into memory. Sounds like common sense, doesn't it?

It helps to also be a minimalist when it comes to session data. Don't store loads of information into the Session object, especially for guest or unauthenticated users. If you're using MemoryStore or using a database like Redis, you can run out of memory. It will take some effort to clog a Redis session store, but if you have a cluster of machines against single-session storage, it's possible.

### Try Out a Real-World Example: connect bodyParser

Let me share an example I found in the connect framework. It was disclosed to the development team and has long since been fixed (as of connect 2.0), so it's not something you have to worry about. But it's still a good example of how memory management should be taken into account.

This is an excerpt of branch 1.x bodyParser middleware in connect:

```
exports.parse['application/x-www-form-urlencoded'] = function(req, options, fn){
    var buf = '';
    req.setEncoding('utf8');
    req.on('data', function(chunk){ buf += chunk });
    req.on('end', function(){
        try {
            req.body = buf.length ? qs.parse(buf) : {};
            fn();
        }
        catch (err) {
            fn(err);
        }
    });
};
```

As you can see, it handles an incoming data request and parses it to the req.body variable. Can you spot the problem?

It's this line: req.on('data', function(chunk){ buf += chunk });.

All the data is collected into an in-memory object before parsing. You have to do that anyway if you plan to present the data to the user, but the problem is that there's no limit to the size of the data. And since this middleware is usually pretty high up in the stack, it doesn't matter who sent the data or which parameters were used if the POST request has the right headers.

The newer versions use the raw-body module for parsing out the body. It checks both the content-length header and the parsed body length on each data event if you give it a limit, and connect by default sets it at 1mb. The whole code is too long to include here—you can find it in GitHub source[5]—but I'll highlight the data handler portion:

```
function onData(chunk) {
    received += chunk.length
    decoder
        ? buffer += decoder.write(chunk)
        : buffer.push(chunk)

    if (limit !== null && received > limit) { // <-- This is what interests us
        if (typeof stream.pause === 'function')
            stream.pause()
        var err = makeError('request entity too large', 'entity.too.large')
        err.status = err.statusCode = 413
        err.received = received
        err.limit = limit
        done(err)
        cleanup()
    }
}
```

As you can see, request handling can have its quirks as well. The size of mistakes you can make in your application regarding resource management depends on your hardware. You're likely not to notice anything until your service goes down.

But the general guideline is to keep the footprint as small and light as possible and always limit the user's input, such as the type of input that can be sent, its size, and specific characters. The less variation you allow in the input, the more likely that it will behave as expected in your program flow.

---

5. https://github.com/stream-utils/raw-body/blob/master/index.js

---

**body-parser**

The bodyParser middleware in Connect was removed as of Connect 3.0. It's split into three separate parsers—urlencoded, json, and multipart —which handle different post data headers accordingly. You should always opt to use the minimum set of these three, to minimize the attack surface.

So instead of using app.use(express.bodyParser()), you can use app.use(bodyParser.urlencoded()), which most likely covers your application's needs. If you do have file uploads, add multipart, and if you're dealing with JSON posts (most likely when you're developing an API), add json.

---

## Avoid Asymmetry in Your Code

Applications are often asymmetric when it comes to client requests. Handling the request is much more resource heavy than making the request. Our Fibonacci example was a good illustration of how it took a long calculation to answer a simple request. Points like these are popular targets for DoS attacks, because by targeting these, attackers can successfully take down a service with limited resources.

You don't want to be an easy target, so you should protect functions that are asymmetrical by limiting access to those functions. One way is to restrict access to the functions to only authenticated users. This way, you can block users who abuse the functions. Another way is to provide a queue system for guest users, where a request is put in the queue and executed only when sufficient resources are available. There are many ways to set up a queue, and I'll demonstrate one way using vasync[6] for our Fibonacci example. First, we set up the function and queue:

```
chp-10-dos/fibonacci-separate-queue.js
// Keep track of jobs and results
var currentRunning = null;
var runningJobs = [];
var unreadResults = {};

// Our calculation function
function fibonacci(obj, cb) {

    // Remove job from queue list
    runningJobs.splice(runningJobs.indexOf(obj.id), 1);
    currentRunning = obj.id;
```

---

6.  https://github.com/davepacheco/node-vasync

```
    // Execute the separate calculation file
    exec('node ' + __dirname + '/fibonacci-calc.js ' + obj.nr,
        function (err, stdout, stderr) {
            //FIXME: We should use execFile
            //FIXME: We should handle possible errors here

            // Insert result to map and continue
            unreadResults[obj.id] = parseInt(stdout);
            currentRunning = false;
            cb();
        });
}

// Create our queue with concurrency 1
var queue = vasync.queuev({
    concurrency: 1,
    worker: fibonacci
});
```

The route handler checks if our job is running or if we have a result:

chp-10-dos/fibonacci-separate-queue.js
```
app.get('/:n*?', function (req, res) {

    var jobId = req.session.jobId;
    if(jobId) {                              // Do we have a running job?
        var result = unreadResults[jobId];
        if(result) {                         // Do we have a result? If so:
            var jobNr = req.session.jobNr;
            delete unreadResults[jobId];   // Free memory

            req.session.jobId = null;
            req.session.jobNr = null;
                                             // Show result to customer
            res.send('Result for ' + jobNr + ' is ' + result);
        } else if(currentRunning === jobId) {
            res.send('Your job is running');
        } else {
            var jobInQueue = (runningJobs.indexOf(jobId) + 1);
            res.send('Your job is ' + jobInQueue + ' in the queue');
        }
        return;
    }

    if(!req.params.n) {
        res.send('Insert number parameter to path');
        return;
    }
```

```
    // Create id for the job and input for our function
    var input = {
        id: Math.random().toString(36).substr(2),
        nr: parseInt(req.params.n)
    };

    queue.push(input);                // Push job to queue
    runningJobs.push(input.id);

    req.session.jobId = input.id;     // Keep tracking info in session
    req.session.jobNr = input.nr;

    if(queue.length() === 0) {
        res.send('Your job is running');
    } else {
        var jobInQueue = (runningJobs.indexOf(jobId) + 1);
        res.send('Your job is ' + jobInQueue + ' in the queue');
    }

});
```

You can see from this example how you can limit the resource usage and make sure no one can use the calculation as a DoS attack point. Of course, attackers can fill up the queue with a ton of jobs and essentially prevent legitimate users from using the function correctly, but that's a case of setting limits. You can limit the size of the number that can be calculated, or how many items can be in the queue at a given time, or even how many requests can come from a single IP address.

We solved the asymmetry problem, though, because no matter how many tasks get dropped into the queue, it still won't kill the server or interfere with other processes.

## Wrapping Up

Denial-of-service attacks target different points of communication between the web server and the client and can be performed in loads of different ways. In this chapter, you learned to avoid using long synchronous functions, storing loads of information in memory, and using heavily asymmetrical functions.

Now that we've educated ourselves about the anti-patterns, we can move forward to securing the client-side application. In the next chapter, we look at one of the most prevalent client-side attacks: XSS.

*The greatness of a nation and its moral progress can be judged by the way its animals are treated. I hold that the more helpless a creature the more entitled it is to protection by man from the cruelty of humankind.*

> *Mahatma Gandhi*

# CHAPTER 11

# Fight Cross-Site Scripts

In the previous chapters we focused on securing our application's server-side code. In this chapter, we shift to the browser and look at the client side to protect the users. We'll look at one of the most common attack vectors on the web: *cross-site scripting* (XSS, and yes, that's how it's written).

An XSS attack executes a malicious script in the targeted person's web browser as if the script was part of the website. There's a place somewhere on the website where user input wasn't properly handled when the page was rendered. Attackers take advantage of the mistake to trick the application into executing their own scripts.

You may think XSS isn't that harmful because it's just a script running in the browser. If so, you aren't thinking broadly enough. Here are some things that can happen if your application is hit with an XSS attack:

- Defacing and content manipulation
- Session hijacking
- Keylogging and other types of information stealing
- Request forgery
- Installation of malicious programs

The most common XSS attack vectors tend to be session hijacking and request forgery because they potentially offer the most monetary gain for attackers. In this chapter, we look at three different types of XSS: reflected, stored, and DOM. You'll learn how to protect your web application with various methods and principles.

## Recognize Different Types of XSS

I said earlier that an XSS attack happens when someone executes his or her own scripts on your page in the context of your web application. Those scripts are running within your website's security space, and the application thinks the site is intentionally running the scripts. How you defend against XSS depends on the type of attack you're facing.

First up is *reflected XSS*, which is a form of XSS where the injected script is reflected off the web server; see the following illustration. This means the script, or reference to the script, is not stored on the server but reflected from somewhere else. This can be either through a form post or a URL parameter.

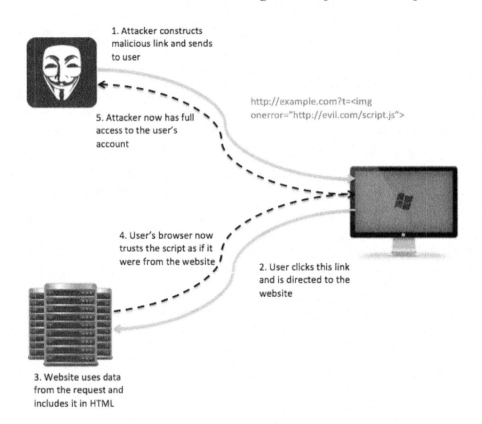

This typically happens because the website's HTML is constructed using URL parameters without proper escaping or validation. Attackers can inject malicious scripts into the HTML and—*voila!*—have access to everything. Well, not quite everything, but a lot.

Google Chrome has introduced an XSS prevention system whereby a script on the page is not executed if it's found in the request query. This greatly limits the reflected XSS attack vector, but don't skip this section just yet. Not all your users will be using Chrome, nor does it solve the issue completely, so stick with it.

The good news is that a reflected XSS attack requires the attacker to provide the link to the victim, which usually raises suspicions in the target. Also the constructed attack links are one off, so they have to convince every victim to visit that specific link.

Compare this to the next type of XSS, *stored XSS*, shown here, where the injected script is stored on the server and executes when rendering the web page. It's frequently stored in the database with user information or content-like comments.

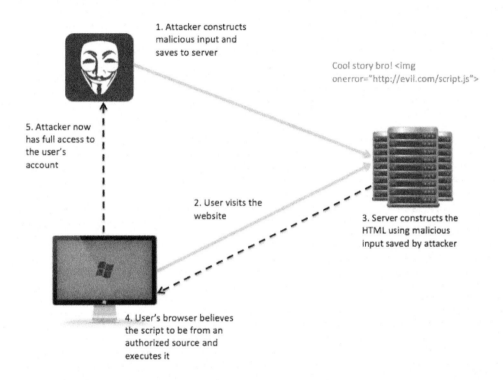

1. Attacker constructs malicious input and saves to server

Cool story bro! <img onerror="http://evil.com/script.js">

5. Attacker now has full access to the user's account

2. User visits the website

3. Server constructs the HTML using malicious input saved by attacker

4. User's browser believes the script to be from an authorized source and executes it

Since stored XSS is already on the server, any user visiting the corresponding page is affected. The attacker doesn't need to apply any phishing or other social engineering methods to direct users to the payload.

*DOM XSS*, shown next, is the least known type of XSS, mainly because it's hard to recognize DOM XSS from stored and reflected attacks. Since DOM XSS targets the browser's interpretation functions, it's considered a client-side execution issue. Reflected and stored XSS are considered server-side execution issues. The following is just one possible example of a DOM XSS.

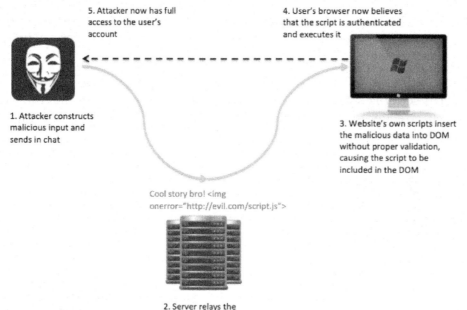

5. Attacker now has full access to the user's account

4. User's browser now believes that the script is authenticated and executes it

1. Attacker constructs malicious input and sends in chat

3. Website's own scripts insert the malicious data into DOM without proper validation, causing the script to be included in the DOM

Cool story bro! <img onerror="http://evil.com/script.js">

2. Server relays the message

DOM XSS has become increasingly relevant in recent years as websites have transitioned toward a heavy client-side architecture with lighter server-side components. This means more and more rendering is happening on the client side, and the server simply serves the data like an API.

Let's see how to protect your users from these different XSS attacks.

## Prevent XSS Through Configuration

Protecting against XSS is a challenge because there are many ways to get around the filters. You can derive large defensive benefits from configuration changes, so let's begin there.

Proper configuration is the most generic, easiest, and often most useful part of mitigating XSS. The following options narrow the XSS vulnerability area and mitigate possible damages caused by malicious scripts.

The first step is to set the HttpOnly flag on cookies. We covered this flag in *Secure the Cookies so No One Can Steal Them*, on page 104. Since the main aim of XSS is to hijack the user's session, the script typically asks for document.cookie containing the sessionID and forwards it to the attacker. If you set the HttpOnly flag on the cookie, then all scripts running on the page are blocked from accessing that cookie.

express and connect session managers turn on the flag by default, so don't disable it. If you're using another framework, remember to set that flag.

---

**Remember to Disable TRACE Calls on Your Server**

While most modern browsers disallow TRACE XMLHttpRequest calls, attackers can still use the method to obtain the session cookie. This is why for extra protection you should disable trace calls on your server.

---

You can also use the *Content Security Policy* (CSP)[1] header on browsers to defend against XSS. The aim of this header is to specify where scripts on the site can originate from. Attackers can inject links to scripts stored on some other server, but those scripts won't be executed because they aren't on the whitelist. It's a good idea to limit the site to serving up content only from the site itself. A basic header to specify this policy is easy:

```
Content-Security-Policy: default-src 'self'
```

We can set the same header by defining the following middleware in our stack:

```
app.use(function (req, res, next) {
    res.header('Content-Security-Policy', "default-src 'self'");
    next();
});
```

For a more nuanced CSP header setup, I recommend you use a module designed for ease of use, such as helmet-csp.[2] It allows defining the headers in a readable manner and sniffs the user-agent to determine the proper header to set. Basic usage is simple:

chp-11-xss/csp.js
```
var csp = require('helmet-csp');

app.use(csp({
    defaultSrc: ["'self'"]
}));
```

However, extending it with various options is also easy and modular:

chp-11-xss/csp-advanced.js
```
app.use(csp({
    // Specify directives as normal
    defaultSrc: ["'self'", 'default.com'],
    scriptSrc: ["'self'", "'unsafe-inline'"],
    styleSrc: ['style.com'],
```

---

1.  https://developer.mozilla.org/en/docs/Security/CSP
2.  https://github.com/helmetjs/csp

```
    imgSrc: ['img.com', 'data:'],
    sandbox: ['allow-forms', 'allow-scripts'],
    reportUri: '/report-violation',

    // Set to an empty array to allow nothing through
    objectSrc: [],

    // Set to true if you only want browsers to report errors, not block them
    reportOnly: false,

    // Set to true if you want to blindly set all headers: Content-Security-Policy,
    // X-WebKit-CSP, and X-Content-Security-Policy.
    setAllHeaders: false,

    // Set to true if you want to disable CSP on Android.
    disableAndroid: false,

    // Set to true if you want to force buggy CSP in Safari 5.1 and below.
    safari5: false
}));
```

If the application has to include scripts from other locations, such as tracking and feedback modules, you will need to list the possible locations in the header. This can quickly grow into a headache. This is why you can use the CSP header in a report only mode, which makes the testing and development much easier.

Before greedily implementing all sorts of configuration options and methods concerning Content Security Policy, refer to the Mozilla page about using CSP[3] for more information.

## Sanitize Input for Reflected/Stored XSS

There's a reason why XSS vulnerabilities are so common in the wild: they're difficult to get rid of. Sanitizing sounds simple in principle, but escaping and disallowing characters can get complicated quickly. Let's look at various rules from the OWASP XSS Prevention Cheat Sheet,[4] which you should keep in mind when building your site.

But first, a small test: in the following code example there's an HTML document—actually, an Embedded JavaScript[5] (EJS) template. Do you know where you could in theory put unsafe content and where you should never put unsafe content?

---

3. https://developer.mozilla.org/en-US/docs/Security/CSP/Using_Content_Security_Policy
4. https://www.owasp.org/index.php/XSS_(Cross_Site_Scripting)_Prevention_Cheat_Sheet
5. http://embeddedjs.com/

```
chp-11-xss/xss-all.ejs
<!DOCTYPE html>
<html>
<head lang="en">
    <meta charset="UTF-8">
    <title>My XSS</title>
    <!--<%- 1 %>-->
    <style>
        body {
            color: #000077;
            font-size: <%- 2 %>;
        }
        <%- 3 %>
    </style>
</head>
<body>
    <nav>
        <<%- 4 %> href="/second">Second page>
        <a href="/third?x=<%- 5 %>">Third page</a>
    </nav>
    <div>
        <div><%- 6 %></div>
        <input <%- 7 %>="nice" value="<%- 8 %>" />

        <button onclick="<%- 9 %>">Touch me</button>
    </div>
    <script>
        var x = '<%- 10 %>';
        <%- 11 %>
    </script>
</body>
</html>
```

Did you find all of them? Are you confident? If not, then keep reading.

It turns out there are some locations in an HTML document where sanitizing is so difficult that you'd be better off avoiding them entirely. Unless, of course, you want attackers to target your customers.

```
chp-11-xss/xss-nono.ejs
<!DOCTYPE html>
<html>
<head lang="en">
    <meta charset="UTF-8">
    <title>My XSS</title>
❶   <!--<%- 1 %>--> <!---->
    <style>
        body {
            color: #000077;
            font-size: large;
        }
```

```
❷          <%- 3 %> <!---->
        </style>
    </head>
    <body>
        <nav>
❸            <<%- 4 %> href="/second">Second page>
            <a href="/third?x=1">Third page</a>
        </nav>
        <div>
            <div>Labeling</div>
❹            <input <%- 7 %>="nice" />

            <button onclick="alert('why')">Touch me</button>
        </div>
        <script>
            var x = 'y';
❺            <%- 11 %> <!---->
        </script>
    </body>
    </html>
```

❶ Inside HTML comments (<%- 1 %>)

❷ Directly inside style attribute (<%- 3 %>)

❸ As a tag name (<%- 4 %>)

❹ As an attribute name (<%- 7 %>)

❺ Directly inside a script attribute (<%- 11 %>)

By avoiding these locations you give your website a fighting chance against XSS. Now let's look at where you potentially can put unsafe data without causing too much harm:

```
chp-11-xss/xss.ejs
<!DOCTYPE html>
<html>
<head lang="en">
    <meta charset="UTF-8">
    <title>My XSS</title>
    <!--Comment-->
    <style>
        body {
            color: #000077;
❶            font-size: <%- 2 %>;
        }
    </style>
</head>
<body>
    <nav>
```

```
        <a href="/second">Second page</a>
②      <a href="/third?x=<%- 5 %>">Third page</a>
    </nav>
    <div>
③      <div><%- 6 %></div>
④      <input value="<%- 8 %>" />

⑤      <button onclick="<%- 9 %>">Touch me</button>
    </div>
    <script>
⑥      var x = '<%- 10 %>';
    </script>
</body>
</html>
```

❶ As CSS values (<%- 2 %>)

❷ As URL parameters (<%- 5 %>)

❸ Inside HTML elements (<%- 6 %>)

❹ Inside common quoted HTML attributes (<%- 8 %>)

❺ Inside JavaScript data values in attributes (<%- 9 %>)

❻ Inside JavaScript data values in script elements (<%- 10 %>)

All of these locations require their own specific form of sanitizing, so we'll go over them one by one. And to be safe you should avoid any other locations not mentioned here unless you do thorough research first and confirm it's okay.

Let's start sanitizing!

---

**node-esapi**

Due to my inability to find context-specific escaping libraries for Node, I've ported the ESAPI4JS (Enterprise Security API for Java-Script) encoder module. This module is called 'node-esapi'.[6] ESAPI4JS was developed by OWASP and implements the escape rules described in this chapter. As such we'll be using it as our sanitizing library in the examples.

---

6.    https://github.com/DeadAlready/node-esapi

## Rule 1: Escape untrusted data inserted into HTML element content.

When you insert data into an HTML body, you have to HTML escape it. This includes normal tags as well, such as div, p, b, and section. Some template engines like jade[7] do this automatically. However, this is absolutely not sufficient for other HTML contexts, and you have to be certain of your template engine if you want to rely on it to handle encoding automatically:

```
<body>...CAN PUT HTML ESCAPED DATA HERE...</body>
<div>...CAN PUT HTML ESCAPED DATA HERE...</div>
etc…
```

You can do this with the ESAPI library:

```
ESAPI.encoder().encodeForHTML(untrustedData);
```

HTML escaping means that you escape the five characters important for XML[8]— &, <, >, ", '—and also the forward slash, /, because it helps end HTML elements. You can use the following conversion table:

```
&   →   &amp;
<   →   &lt;
>   →   &gt;
"   →   &quot;
'   →   &#x27;      &apos; not recommended because it's not in the HTML spec.
/   →   &#x2F;
```

## Rule 1.1: Sanitize HTML markup with a library designed for the job.

When your application lets users enter HTML content, you can't just trust it, but you can't simply use encoding because it would break the HTML. Use the library designed for the task.

Several different modules in Node.js were written specifically for this purpose; I will highlight two of them:

- Bleach[9]: designed for easy HTML sanitizing. It supports both whitelist and blacklist sanitizing and has other options as well. Unfortunately this module hasn't been updated for over a year.
- Sanitizer[10]: a port of the Caja-HTML-Sanitizer.[11] It's a thorough HTML sanitizer developed by Google that also supports various options.

---

7.   https://github.com/visionmedia/jade
8.   http://en.wikipedia.org/wiki/XML
9.   https://github.com/ecto/bleach
10.  https://github.com/theSmaw/Caja-HTML-Sanitizer
11.  https://code.google.com/p/google-caja/source/browse/trunk/src/com/google/caja/plugin/html-sanitizer.js

## Rule 2: Escape untrusted data inserted into HTML attributes.

When you insert untrusted data into common HTML attributes like value, width, and name, you have to encode accordingly. Surround the attribute value with either single or double quotes:

```
<!-- inside single quoted attribute -->
<div attr='...CAN PUT ATTRIBUTE ESCAPED DATA HERE...'>content</div>

<!-- inside double quoted attribute -->
<div attr="...CAN PUT ATTRIBUTE ESCAPED DATA HERE...">content</div>
```

The following shows how to apply the rule with the ESAPI library:

```
ESAPI.encoder().encodeForHTMLAttributes(untrustedData);
```

When escaping for HTML attributes you need to escape all characters, except for alphanumeric characters, with ASCII values less than 256 with the &#xHH; format (or a named entity if available) to prevent switching out of the attribute.

The reason this rule is so broad is that developers frequently leave attributes unquoted. Properly quoted attributes can only be escaped with the corresponding quote. Unquoted attributes, however, can be broken out of with many characters, including \ [space] % * + , - / ; < = > ^ and |.

This rule does not cover complex attributes like href, src, style or any event handler like onclick. Event handler attributes follow rule 3.

## Rule 3: Escape untrusted data inserted into JavaScript data values.

This rule applies to dynamically created JavaScript code—both script blocks and event handlers. The only place to put data in this case is in the quoted data values. Any other JavaScript context is dangerous—it's easy to switch execution context, because there are many characters that allow the attacker to do so:

```
<!-- We might expect a string -->
<script>alert(<%- userValue %>)</script>

<!-- And instead get -->
<script>alert(confirm('have you been xssd?'))</script>
```

Always *quote data values* because it drastically limits the possible context escape values attackers could use:

```
<!-- inside a quoted string -->
<script>alert('...CAN PUT JAVASCRIPT ESCAPED DATA HERE...')</script>
```

```
<!-- one side of a quoted expression -->
<script>x='...CAN PUT JAVASCRIPT ESCAPED DATA HERE...'</script>

<!-- inside quoted event handler -->
<div onclick="x='...CAN PUT JAVASCRIPT ESCAPED DATA HERE...'"></div>
```

Some JavaScript functions can never safely use untrusted data as input, as shown here:

```
window.setInterval('...EVEN IF YOU ESCAPE UNTRUSTED DATA YOU ARE XSSED HERE...');
```

You can encode for JavaScript using the ESAPI library:

```
ESAPI.encoder().encodeForJS(untrustedData);
//or
ESAPI.encoder().encodeForJavaScript(untrustedData);
//or
ESAPI.encoder().encodeForJavascript(untrustedData);
```

When escaping for JavaScript you need to escape all characters, except for alphanumeric characters less than 256, with the &#xHH; format to prevent switching out of the data value into the script context or into another attribute.

*Do not* use any escaping shortcuts like \\" because the quote character will wind up being matched by the HTML attribute parser, which runs first. Escaping shortcuts are also susceptible to escape-the-escape attacks, where the attacker sends \\" and the vulnerable code turns that into \\\\" to enable the quote.

If an event handler is properly quoted, breaking out requires you to have the corresponding quote. This rule is intentionally broad because event handler attributes are often left unquoted. Unquoted attributes can be broken out of with many characters, including \ [space] % * + , - / ; < = > ^ and |.

Also, a </ script> closing tag will close a script block even though it's inside a quoted string because the HTML parser runs before the JavaScript parser.

## Rule 3.1: Escape JSON values in an HTML context and read the data with JSON.parse.

In Web 2.0 applications you often generate data by the application and transfer it through JSON. The data can be received with AJAX calls, but that's not always efficient. You often load an initial block of JSON on the page to act as the base data. Let's look at how you can do this securely.

First of all, when asking for JSON data from the server, ensure that the HTTP Content-Type header is set correctly to application/json so that the browser doesn't accidentally try to interpret the content as HTML.

With express, this is handled automatically when you send a response with res.json() instead of res.send(), because it sets the header internally:

```
app.get('/json', function (req, res) {
    res.json({my:'awesome JSON'});
});
```

A common anti-pattern when serving JSON as part of the original HTML looks like the following:

```
<script>
    var initData = <%- JSON.stringify(data) %>;
    // WARNING! This is not a recommended approach as it
    // is vulnerable without proper escaping
</script>
```

The problem with this approach is that it's possible to change the execution context, because the HTML interpreter runs before the JavaScript interpreter. Instead, I recommend that you separate the server-side data without breaching context barriers. Place JSON into HTML as a normal element and then use JavaScript to parse the contents:

```
<script id="init_data" type="application/json">
    <%= ESAPI.encoder().encodeForHTML(JSON.stringify(data)) %>
</script>
<script>
    var dataElement = document.getElementById('init_data');
    var jsonText = dataElement.textContent || dataElement.innerText

    // Always use JSON.parse instead of eval
    var initData = JSON.parse(jsonText);
</script>
```

## Rule 4: Escape and validate untrusted data inserted into CSS property values.

Although it might not seem like it, CSS (Cascading Style Sheets) can be used as an XSS attack vector because CSS can execute and include scripts. Here's an example of how CSS is used in an attack:

```
{ background-url : "javascript:alert(1)"; }  // and all other URLs
{ text-size: "expression(alert('XSS'))"; }    // only in IE
```

When you use untrusted data to construct CSS or set style properties on elements, make sure you perform proper validation checks. Don't use untrusted data for anything other than property values. Don't put untrusted data into complex property values such as url and behavior. I suggest also avoiding the Internet Explorer–specific expression property since it allows JavaScript.

```
<style>selector { property : ...CAN PUT CSS ESCAPED DATA HERE...; } </style>
```

```
<style>selector { property : "...CAN PUT CSS ESCAPED DATA HERE..."; } </style>
```

```
<span style="property : ...CAN PUT CSS ESCAPED DATA HERE...">text</span>
```

Even if you escape CSS, you still have to ensure all URLs start with http: or https: and not with javascript:. Property values should never start with expression.

Here's the same example, using the ESAPI library:

```
ESAPI.encoder().encodeForCSS(untrustedData);
```

When escaping for CSS, remember to escape all characters, except for alphanumeric characters, with ASCII values less than 256 with the &#xHH; escaping format. As mentioned in a previous rule, *do not* use any escaping shortcuts like \" because the quote character may be matched by the HTML attribute parser instead. These shortcuts are also susceptible to escape-the-escape attacks where \\" turns into \\\\".

If an attribute is quoted, breaking out requires the corresponding quote. All attributes should be quoted, but your encoding should be strong enough to prevent XSS when untrusted data is placed in unquoted contexts.

Unquoted attributes can be broken out of with many characters, including \ [space] % * + , - / ; < = > ^ and |. Also, the </ style> tag will close the style block even though it's inside a quoted string because the HTML parser runs before the CSS parser.

Please note that aggressive CSS encoding and validation are recommended to prevent XSS attacks for both quoted and unquoted attributes.

### Rule 5: Escape untrusted data inserted into HTML URL parameter values.

This is one of the easiest rules to apply. When you want to put data into HTTP GET parameters, URL escape it!

```
<a href="http://www.somesite.com?test=...CAN PUT URL ESCAPED DATA HERE...">link</a>
```

You can do this easily with the ESAPI library:

```
ESAPI.encoder().encodeForURL(untrustedData);
```

When escaping for URL, escape all characters, except for alphanumeric characters, with ASCII values less than 256 with the %HH escaping format. Don't include untrusted data in data: URLs because there's no good way to disable those attacks with escaping.

All attributes should be quoted. Unquoted attributes can be broken out of with many characters, including \ [space] % * + , - / ; < = > ^ and |. Note that entity encoding is useless in this context.

Be careful with URL encoding and relative URLs. If the user input is meant to be placed into href or src or other URL-based attributes, then it should be validated beforehand to make sure it doesn't point to an unexpected protocol or script file. After that, encode URLs based on context, like all other data.

For example, when inserting into a href attribute, you *attribute* encode it.

## How All the Rules Come Together

To avoid XSS attacks when rendering templates on the server side, you should always be careful with unsafe content. You must encode depending on the location where the content is being inserted. Using the wrong encoding format doesn't help you, and there's no one-size-fits-all rule that you can apply. Look at the following example to see how you can combine all the methods in one place:

```
chp-11-xss/xss-encoded.ejs
<!DOCTYPE html>
<html>
<head lang="en">
    <meta charset="UTF-8">
    <title>My XSS</title>
    <!--This is going to be great-->
    <% var E = ESAPI.encoder() %>
    <style>
        body {
            color: #000077;
            font-size: <%- E.encodeForCSS(unsafe); %>;
        }
    </style>
</head>
<body>
    <nav>
        <a href="/second?x=<%- E.encodeForURL(unsafe); %>">Second page</a>
    </nav>
    <div>
        <h1><%- E.encodeForHTML(unsafe); %></h1>
        <input value="<%- E.encodeForHTMLAttributes(unsafe); %>" />
```

```
        <button onclick="<%- E.encodeForJS(unsafe); %>">Touch me</button>
    </div>
    <script id="json" type="application/json">
      <%- E.encodeForHTML(JSON.stringify(data)) %>
    </script>

    <script>
        var x = '<%- E.encodeForJS(unsafe); %>';
        var json = JSON.parse(document.getElementById('json').innerHTML);
    </script>
</body>
</html>
```

# Sanitize Input for DOM XSS

DOM-based XSS is a different beast altogether, and it deserves its own section and rules. To get a thorough overview of DOM XSS and sanitizing rules, consult the OWASP DOM-based XSS Prevention Cheat Sheet.[12] Also, if you skipped the previous section on various sanitizing rules, then go back. You need to know how to deal with first-order XSS attacks to understand how to deal with DOM XSS.

If you're using a lot of DOM manipulation in your application, it's prone to DOM XSS. I recommend using a JavaScript validation library designed for context-specific validations, such as the ESAPI JavaScript library[13] from OWASP.

Treat DOM-based XSS sanitizing as a two-step challenge. First, you get the data into a JavaScript variable, as I discussed previously in *Rule 3: Escape untrusted data inserted into JavaScript data values.*, on page 149. Then, you sanitize the data according to the usage.

If you used only the previous rules, you'd wind up with something like the following:

chp-11-xss/xss-dom-simple.ejs
```
<!DOCTYPE html>
<html>
<head lang="en">
    <meta charset="UTF-8">
    <title>My DOM XSS</title>
</head>
<body>
    <div id="dynamic"></div>
    <script>
```

---

12. https://www.owasp.org/index.php/DOM_based_XSS_Prevention_Cheat_Sheet
13. https://code.google.com/p/owasp-esapi-js/

```
        // Step 1 - Get data
        var text = '<%- ESAPI.encoder().encodeForJS(unsafe) %>';

        // Step 2 - Use data
        var $element = document.getElementById('dynamic');
        $element.innerHTML = text; // <- VULNERABLE! We need HTML encoding
    </script>
</body>
</html>
```

You can fix this by applying reverse encoding on the data-insertion part:

chp-11-xss/xss-dom-simple-fix1.ejs
```
<!DOCTYPE html>
<html>
<head lang="en">
    <meta charset="UTF-8">
    <title>My DOM XSS</title>
</head>
<body>
    <div id="dynamic"></div>
    <script>
        <% var E = ESAPI.encoder(); %>
        // Step 1 - Get data
        // Apply reverse order encoding
        var text = '<%- E.encodeForJS(E.encodeForHTML(unsafe)) %>';

        // Step 2 - Use data
        var $element = document.getElementById('dynamic');
        $element.innerHTML = text;
    </script>
</body>
</html>
```

You can also apply encoding at runtime:

chp-11-xss/xss-dom-simple-fix2.ejs
```
<!DOCTYPE html>
<html>
<head lang="en">
    <meta charset="UTF-8">
    <title>My DOM XSS</title>
    <script src="/esapi/esapi.js"></script>
    <script src="/esapi/resources/i18n/ESAPI_Standard_en_US.properties.js"></script>
    <script src="/esapi/resources/Base.esapi.properties.js"></script>
</head>
<body>
    <div id="dynamic"></div>
    <script>
        org.owasp.esapi.ESAPI.initialize();
```

```
            // Step 1 - Get data
            var text = '<%- ESAPI.encoder().encodeForJS(unsafe) %>';

            // Step 2 - Use data
            var $element = document.getElementById('dynamic');
            // Encode using client side script
            $element.innerHTML = $ESAPI.encoder().encodeForHTML(text);
    </script>
</body>
</html>
```

Unfortunately, you can't just use the corresponding level of encoding from the previous section when dealing with DOM XSS. The rules are slightly different, so let's take a look.

### Rule 0: Use DOM construction methods instead of HTML interpretation.

Untrusted data should be treated only as displayable text. You should never treat untrusted data as code or markup within JavaScript code. In order to construct dynamic HTML interfaces, you should use JavaScript methods designed to construct DOM, such as document.createElement("..."), element.setAttribute("...","value"), and element.appendChild(...). Don't build HTML strings and let the browser interpret them for you.

You don't have to have a complex environment that's hard to escape properly, so instead of this

```
// Get value
var text = '<%- ESAPI.encoder().encodeForJS(unsafe) %>';
// Construct HTML
var input = '<input name="company_name" value="' + text + '" />';

// Insert HTML
var form1 = document.forms[0];
form1.insertAdjacentHTML('beforeend', input);

// or with jquery
$('form:first').append(input);
```

use DOM methods to remove an interpretation layer and simplify the process:

```
// Get value
var text = '<%- ESAPI.encoder().encodeForJS(unsafe) %>';
// Construct HTML
var input = document.createElement('input');
input.setAttribute('name', 'company_name');
input.setAttribute('value', text);

// Insert HTML
var form1 = document.forms[0];
```

```
form1.insertAdjacentHTML('beforeend', input);

// or with jquery
$('form:first').append(input);
```

The element.setAttribute() is safe for only a limited number of attributes. Dangerous attributes include any attributes that are for a command execution context, such as onclick() or onblur().

## Rule 1: JavaScript and HTML encode before HTML subcontext.

Several methods in JavaScript can directly render HTML. When providing untrusted input to these methods, you first have to be sure that it doesn't break out of the JavaScript context and the HTML context. You can do this by applying the encoding backwards, so you first deal with HTML encoding and then JavaScript encoding. The following list shows some examples of methods used for HTML rendering:

```
element.innerHTML = "<HTML> Tags and markup";
element.outerHTML = "<HTML> Tags and markup";
document.write("<HTML> Tags and markup");
document.writeln("<HTML> Tags and markup");
```

Here's an example of how you can encode using ESAPI and EJS for server-side template rendering:

```
<%
var htmlEncoded = ESAPI.encoder().encodeForHTML(unsafe);
var jsEncoded = ESAPI.encoder().encodeForJS(htmlEncoded);
%>
element.innerHTML = "<%- jsEncoded %>";
```

If you get the data directly from the server, such as when you're using AJAX to get the data for the client side, you can use the following example:

```
element.innerHTML = $ESAPI.encoder().encodeForHTML(unsafe);
```

## Rule 2: Do not apply attribute encoding in DOM context.

When you're inserting untrusted input into an attribute value, then you don't have to *attribute* escape it from within the DOM context. You just have to worry about JavaScript escape. Using both will break how the value is visually represented. Let's go over some bad examples, so you know what you shouldn't do:

```
var x = document.createElement("input");
x.setAttribute("name", "company_name");
// In the following line of code, companyName represents untrusted user input
// The Encoder.encodeForHTMLAttr() is unnecessary and causes double-encoding
```

```
<%
var attEncoded = ESAPI.encoder().encodeForHTMLAttr(companyName);
var jsEncoded = ESAPI.encoder().encodeForJS(attEncoded);
%>
x.setAttribute("value", '<%- jsEncoded %>');
var form1 = document.forms[0];
form1.appendChild(x);
```

If companyName had the value Johnson & Johnson, you would see Johnson \&amp; Johnson in the input text field. In this case, you should use only JavaScript encoding to prevent an attacker from closing out the single quotes and inserting code or escaping to HTML and opening a new <script> tag. Let's do this correctly by encoding only for JavaScript:

```
var x = document.createElement("input");
x.setAttribute("name", "company_name");
x.setAttribute("value", '<%- ESAPI.encoder().encodeForJS(companyName) %>');
var form1 = document.forms[0];
form1.appendChild(x);
```

### Rule 3: Avoid execution subcontexts.

I recommend that you don't insert untrusted data into event handlers and JavaScript subcontexts. OWASP just says to be very careful, but why take the risk? You should find another way to do what you want instead. The JavaScript interpreter works a bit differently and often doesn't stop attacks within the context. For various examples on how this can fail, you can look at the OWASP DOM XSS Cheat Sheet Rule 3.[14]

### Rule 4: Do not apply CSS encoding in style context.

When manipulating style with JavaScript and untrusted data, you don't have to worry about breaking out of the CSS context. Even though you don't have to CSS encode the data beforehand, you still need to worry about unsafe CSS properties. Remember that you should never let unsafe data specify which property gets changed. It's always better to use a whitelist instead. You should also make sure URLs don't have execution context within them, and don't accept expression or such values in the property.

### Rule 5: JavaScript and URL encode when creating links.

This rule is similar to rule 5 for regular XSS attacks but also includes the JavaScript encoding layer:

---

14. https://www.owasp.org/index.php/DOM_based_XSS_Prevention_Cheat_Sheet#RULE_.233_-_Be_Careful_when_Inserting_Untrusted_Data_into_the_Event_Handler_and_JavaScript_code_Subcontexts_within_an_Execution_Context

```
<%
var urlEncoded = ESAPI.encoder().encodeForURL(userRelativePath);
var jsEncoded = ESAPI.encoder().encodeForJS(urlEncoded);
%>
var href = '<%- jsEncoded %>';
var x = document.createElement("a");
x.setAttribute("href", href);
var y = document.createTextElement("Click Me To Test");
x.appendChild(y);
document.body.appendChild(x);
```

### Different Steps of DOM XSS Protection

The DOM level adds another layer of interpretation to the data you have to protect. When constructing scripts dynamically, you must use double encoding or use client-side encoding appropriate to the subcontext to protect the layers.

You need to handle two steps of DOM XSS protection. The first step is to get the data into a variable. You can JavaScript encode if you're constructing the script on the service side. You can also transfer the value as JSON and use JSON.parse to interpret it. I cannot emphasize enough that using eval() would be a terrible idea.

The second step involves how you use the data. When you're inserting the data into an HTML or URL context, you need to encode accordingly. But if you're inserting the data in an attribute or CSS context, you should not encode. As discussed previously, you need to avoid dangerous properties, though.

And above all, you should avoid inserting data into a JavaScript subcontext.

# Wrapping Up

In this chapter we covered a whopping amount of information about XSS. Its large attack surface makes it difficult to evade, but you now know the various OWASP rules on how to avoid XSS flaws in your application. You should be able to identify different attack points and know when to apply which encoding rules.

XSS is not the only attack vector on the client side. In the next chapter, we look at another one: CSRF (cross-site request forgery).

CHAPTER 12

# Avoid Request Forgery

In the previous chapter we looked at XSS, one of the most widely used client-side attacks. In this chapter, we look at another client-side attack: *cross-site request forgery* (CSRF).

Cross-site request forgery, also known as *one-click attack* or *session riding*, is an attack that makes unauthorized requests on the behalf of a trusted user. Whereas XSS exploits the user's trust, CSRF exploits the site's trust in the user's browser, as illustrated in the following figure.

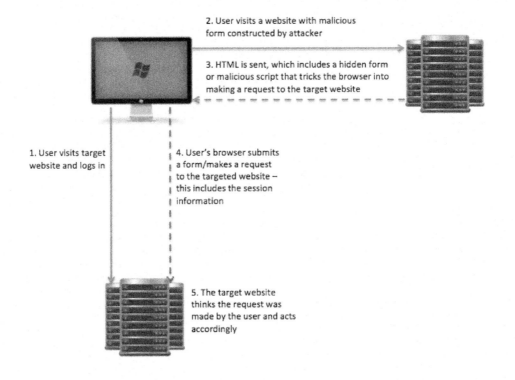

Attackers use this method to modify the target website, and as far as the application is concerned, the trusted user is the one executing those commands. CSRF is popular because the attackers don't need to compromise the web application at all. Attackers can set up their own malicious website or take over some other application and lure victims to those sites.

CSRF is highly effective, and it's even more so when it targets administrative accounts to get higher levels of access.

In this chapter we look at the logic on how to defend against CSRF and then discuss different ways to apply the logic. We don't want our users to worry about their accounts being abused while browsing online.

## Follow the Logic to Protect Against CSRF

Cross-site request forgery requires the site to trust the browser. Attackers abuse this trust by making the browser submit legitimate-looking requests to the web application. We fight this by adding *watermarks*, or things attackers can't forge, so that the site can differentiate between legitimate and forged requests.

In a CSRF attack, the attacker forces the browser to make a request. Attackers can't do that via AJAX because browsers by default don't allow cross-origin requests. Thus, CSRF is a blind attack, similar to blind SQL injection discussed in *Avoid SQL Injection Attacks*, on page 61. Attackers can make the requests but will typically not see the responses.

By default, websites can't make requests to other websites from scripts running on the page. New web standards allow websites to send *Cross-Origin Resource Sharing* (CORS)[1] headers to override this policy. CORS headers let websites specify other domains that can make requests via scripts, along with any methods and restrictions that may apply. You can build more complex web services, but using CORS with loose settings seriously undermines your website security. If you're using CORS, be sure to minimize the permissions you allow!

With CSRF, the attacker wants to modify the state of the website in some way, so unless you allowed CORS, you don't have to worry about information requests. You can focus on modifying requests.

I recommend using POST, PATCH, and PUT requests to handle all state-modifying processes such as insert, delete, and update. The data can be inserted in the

---

1.  https://developer.mozilla.org/en-US/docs/Web/HTTP/Access_control_CORS

body of the request, which is encrypted if you're using SSL. That takes care of the eavesdropper problem. POST, PATCH, and PUT are also written in HTTP standards.

Why not use GET? Consider that search engines issue GET requests to links that they find. You wouldn't want those requests to be able to change something in your application's state.

To prevent CSRF attacks, you have three choices: to add something to the request attackers do not know, have the browser add something the attackers can't change, or have users add something manually when making the request. Of the choices, the most secure is to have a challenge-response system where the submission form requires the user to take part. This could be a CAPTCHA image or a request to re-authenticate. This way, the application issues a challenge that can't be forged programmatically. Unfortunately, this approach causes a bad user experience and is difficult to implement to boot, so we'll explore some alternatives.

Let's begin with the first and most widely used system of CSRF protection—the synchronized token pattern.

## Synchronize Your Tokens as Part of CSRF Protection

The most common CSRF protection is randomly generating a token for the form or session and always including it as part of a POST request. Every request is validated by comparing the submitted value with the expected token value. If the values match, the request is valid. There are several modules to choose from, but we'll take a look at csurf,[2] which used to be part of express.

```
app.use(cookieParser());
app.use(session({
    secret: 'this is a nice secret',
    resave: false,
    saveUninitialized: true
}));
app.use(bodyParser.urlencoded());
app.use(csurf()); // Include csurf middleware

// Show form
app.get('/', function (req, res, next) {
    var form = '<form method="POST" action="/add">' +
        '<input type="hidden" name="_csrf" value="' +
        req.csrfToken() + '" />' + // add hidden token field
        '<input type="text" name="name" placeholder="name" />' +
        '<input type="text" name="value" placeholder="value" />' +
```

---

2. https://github.com/expressjs/csurf

```
    '<input type="submit" value="Submit" />' +
    '</form>';

  res.send(form);
});
```

It took just two lines of code to set up protection from CSRF. While the attacker can construct and send a POST request, he or she won't be able to set a valid _csrf token.

Fortunately, csurf handles the heavy lifting and allows you to send the token as a _csrf field in the POST or GET request. You can also use the HTTP header X-CSRF-Token.

You're not finished yet. You should add logging to keep track of malicious activity against your site. csurf provides a specific error code you can use in your logging code.

```
// error handler
app.use(function (err, req, res, next) {
    if (err.code !== 'EBADCSRFTOKEN') {
        return next(err) // some other error
    }

    // handle CSRF token errors here

    // Besides just saying that we had a mismatch
    // we should log some useful information about the request here
    // like the user and referrer and origin headers of the request for example
    console.warn('CSRF token mismatch');

    res.status(403)
    res.send('form tampered with')
})
```

This form of CSRF protection is easy to implement and effective, but it requires the application to save the state into the session. This is troublesome if the application grows big enough. Depending on the session storage system you're using, it can take up too much memory or cause issues in clusters if sessions keep going to the same machine. So if you don't want to deal with saving sessions, you can work with cookies instead.

## Double-Submit the Cookie to Prevent CSRF Attacks

This defense technique isn't all that different from the previous one, except the _csrf token doesn't get stored in the session. Instead, you add the token to the site's cookies. The idea is to submit the token in the body of the request along with the cookie so that they can be compared. If the values match, it's a legitimate request.

This method simply moves the location of the token from the session to the cookie as you switch from server-side defense to client-side defense. Instead of taking up storage, you now take up bandwidth. You can do this simply with csurf middleware:

```
app.use(cookieParser());
app.use(bodyParser.urlencoded());

// Include csurf middleware, with cookie option
app.use(csurf({cookie: true}));

// Show form
app.get('/', function (req, res, next) {
    var form = '<form method="POST" action="/add">' +
        '<input type="hidden" name="_csrf" value="' +
        req.csrfToken() + '" />' + // add hidden token field
        '<input type="text" name="name" placeholder="name" />' +
        '<input type="text" name="value" placeholder="value" />' +
        '<input type="submit" value="Submit" />' +
        '</form>';

    res.send(form);
});
```

The extra bandwidth from sending the token back and forth with every request can be a drawback. Which method you wind up using would depend entirely on your application.

Synchronized token patterns are the most commonly used method to prevent CSRF, but there are other ways that don't require extra tokens. We look at them in the next section.

## O Request, Where Art Thou From?

There may be a reason why you don't want to use tokens for CSRF protection, such as having a stateless setup or not wanting to use a lot of resources. Perhaps the application doesn't have strict security requirements. For any of these situations, you can just use the standard information the browser includes in a typical request.

Modern browsers send Referer and Origin headers with requests when navigating through links or submitting forms on a web page. They give the application information about which page the request originated from and can be used for both tracking and CSRF protection. You can look at the headers to determine if the form did originate on your site.

Attackers can spoof headers if they're creating the requests, but it's pretty much impossible to do so when submitting a request via the victim's browser. These headers can be checked for consistency since if the requests originated from a different domain, the browser will tell you that upfront.

On an important note, the Referer header isn't sent when the request originates from an HTTPS site. The Origin header was specifically created to mitigate that shortcoming, so you should prefer to use that.

Let's create our own CSRF middleware to check these headers:

```
chp-12-csrf/header-middleware.js
'use strict';

var url = require('url');

module.exports = function getCsrf(domainData) {
    if(typeof domainData !== 'object') {
        throw new TypeError('Expected an object');
    }

    // Function for validating the origin header
    function validate(origin) {
        var data = url.parse(origin);
        if(typeof data !== 'object') {
            return false;
        }
        // Match against the provided data
        return !Object.keys(domainData).some(function (key) {
            if(data[key] !== domainData[key]) {
                console.log(data[key], domainData[key]);
                return true;
            }
        });
    }

    // Define ignored methods
    var ignoredMethods = ['GET', 'HEAD', 'OPTIONS'];

    return function csrf(req, res, next) {

        // ignore speficied methods
        if (ignoredMethods.indexOf(req.method) !== -1) {
            next();
            return;
        }
```

```
    var origin = req.headers.origin || req.headers.referer;

    // Validate the header
    if(!origin || !validate(origin)) {
        var error = new Error('Unauthorized');
        error.code = 403;
        // Besides just saying that we had a mismatch
        // we should log some useful information about the request here
        // the user and referrer and origin headers of the request for example
        console.warn('Origin/Referer mismatch');
        next(error);
        return;
    }

    // Everything ok, so continue
    next();
  };
};
```

We can set up this middleware to validate any value returned by url.parse. In this case we're most interested in the protocol, host, hostname, and port variables. The next example just checks for hostname and port. If the hostname or port differs from localhost:3000, the application will throw errors:

```
var csrf = require('./csrf');
app.use(csrf({
    hostname: 'localhost',
    port: '3000'
}));
```

While this method of CSRF protection is resource friendly, it depends on the browser to send correct headers. There can be consistency issues since not all browsers behave the same, and some don't always include the headers in requests. That's the downside of using this approach.

## Avoid Setting Up Common CSRF Pitfalls in Your Code

express makes it easy to implement CSRF protections, but there are some pitfalls with using express and existing middleware. In this section, we look at three such issues.

The first issue is the middleware methodOverride in express, which lets you implement or modify the application's RESTful behavior. For example, you just add a _method parameter to do a DELETE request with a body or use a simple form to create a PUT request. Unfortunately, the middleware interferes with CSRF protection.

The standard practice in most CSRF prevention methods is to ignore GET, OPTIONS, and HEAD request methods. The GET request should be used just to obtain information and should not modify data. However, if the server is using methodOverride after middleware for CSRF protection, then it becomes possible to send a GET request with the parameter _method=POST.

```
app.use(express.urlencoded());
app.use(express.csrf());
app.use(express.methodOverride());
...
```

The GET request will be ignored by CSRF protection middleware, but it will still be handled by POST routes and let attackers bypass the defenses you've put in place.

CSRF doesn't just target authenticated users. It's a common misperception that only forms located in the authenticated areas of the site need CSRF protection. While damage done by unauthenticated forms tends to be on a smaller scale, you still don't want it to happen on your site.

Consider login forms. The attacker can't use the victim's session because the user hasn't logged in yet, but here's a possible attack scenario: the attacker can set up an unauthorized account on the site, log into that account using the victim's browser, and hope the victim doesn't notice that it's the wrong account. The attacker can later harvest any sensitive information the victim generated in that account. While a circumstantial attack, it can be effective in situations where user history is logged or users upload media for later use.

These unvalidated forms can also be used to perform more sophisticated attacks like BREACH[3] to compromise the user's session and gain access. Don't underestimate the ingenuity of attackers; protect all your forms.

When dealing with logged-out users, session-based token patterns can cause problems too, depending on how the application was designed. For areas of the site where users aren't logged in, I highly recommend using either header-checking or double-submit cookies with tokens unrelated to the session.

It is *crucial* that you to protect your application from XSS. If you skipped Chapter 11, *Fight Cross-Site Scripts*, on page 139, then go back and read it now, because all the CSRF protections (except some challenge-response systems) can be defeated easily if the application has an unpatched XSS vulnerability. If the attacker can execute JavaScript under the application's domain, it can make requests with the correct Referer and/or Origin headers. The

---

3.    https://en.wikipedia.org/wiki/BREACH_(security_exploit)

attacker would also be able to get the necessary tokens to make the request look legitimate.

While XSS cannot directly bypass challenge-response systems because the questions require user interaction, the attacker could use the XSS vulnerability to trick the user into answering the challenge. Bypassing challenge-response systems with CSS is typically difficult to do if the methods are implemented properly.

If you hope to defeat CSRF, then you need to first master XSS.

## Wrapping Up

In this chapter we studied CSRF, and you learned how this attack can be used to target your website. It's a dangerous attack vector because the attacker can use a different website or social engineering to perform different functions on the site. We also covered token- and header-based defenses, which can be very effective. But you saw how these methods turn out to be useless if you don't address XSS issues first.

We've looked at a lot of ways you can secure your code. In the next chapter, we'll look at how you can also secure your and your clients' data.

*Only trust thyself, and another shall not betray thee.*

> ➤ *William Penn*

# CHAPTER 13

# Protect Your Data

In previous chapters, you learned how to protect your database from injection and concurrency attacks. When your application is dealing with sensitive information such as credit card numbers or medical records, you have to take even more steps to make sure the data is secure.

Attackers value credit card numbers and medical information—it's their gold. Despite what you may think or stories you may have heard, most cybercriminals are not looking for lulz—they're after money.

In this chapter, we step up our game so that you can protect your data in such a way that stealing it would be a long and complex process. You want the criminal to give up and go away. We'll start by looking at how data flows to your application so that you can identify the points of attack and then move on to mitigation techniques.

## Understand Your Application's Data Flow

Before you can protect user information stored in your application, you have to know what kind of data you even have and then figure out which data needs protecting. The illustration on page 172 shows the main components involved in data transfer from the user to your server.

The data flow begins with the client application asking the user to provide some data. Once the user enters something (or does something in the application), the browser sends the collected information over the network to the server. The server validates the data it received, performs some magic, and pushes it into storage for later use.

Very straightforward, right? But attackers can target several points in the data flow to intercept some of that information flowing between the user and

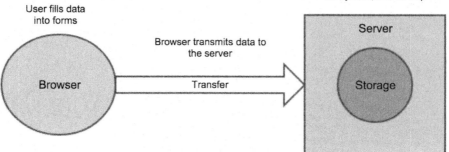

the server. The illustration on page 173 shows some of the possible ways attackers target the data flow.

First, attackers can use XSS (cross-site scripting) attacks against the client application. Attackers who can access the user's system can also target the browser's caching system. Be wary of XSS attacks, which we covered back in Chapter 11, *Fight Cross-Site Scripts*, on page 139.

Next, look at how data is being transferred from the client to the server, because it can be attacked just like any other data transfer. Here's where our HTTPS setup, which we covered in *Use TLS and SSL to Secure Your Connections*, on page 25 pays off. There are also some nuances to be aware of when the data reaches the server.

Finally, think about storage. You've already learned how to protect the application from injection attacks. But it takes only one mistake to cost you the whole database holding all the information. You can't hash user data the way you hash passwords because the application needs to be able to work with the data. So you encrypt the data while it's in storage and decrypt the information when you need it.

Keep in mind where the weak spots can be found in your data flow while we look at how you can add layers of protection around each point.

## Protect the Client Application and Data

Let's start with the client application. We're going to skip how to educate and protect the user because that's a whole different task and a topic for another

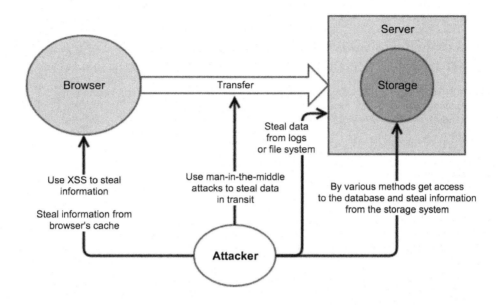

book. We'll start from the source of the data and work our way through to when it reaches the server.

XSS and caching attacks are among the most popular attacks at this point. We look at XSS in great detail in its own chapter Chapter 11, *Fight Cross-Site Scripts*, on page 139, so we won't dig into this attack vector here. Since XSS is a popular attack method, you need to go through the XSS chapter to protect your users.

Browsers rely on caches and autocomplete tools to speed up web browsing and help users accomplish more things while doing less work. Although useful, they also create opportunities for attackers.

Autocomplete in browsers lets users quickly fill out different forms with the same pieces of information. Think about how saving the shipping address information from one form saves time and effort the next time you buy something. To be able to autocomplete forms, the browser first needs to store the data somewhere. The thing is, attackers can trick the browser into displaying that information at the wrong time.

Imagine a situation where the computer has multiple users. One user enters some sensitive information in a form and submits it. Another user comes along, opens the same page, and sees the sensitive information when autocomplete fills out the form. This is a simple example, but you can see why saving sensitive information this way would be bad.

When dealing with forms collecting sensitive information, you should either turn off autocomplete entirely, as shown in this example, or be more selective:

```
<form method="POST" action="/saveData" autocomplete="off">
    <input type="text" name="sensitive" />
    <input type="submit" value="Submit" />
</form>
```

To be more selective you can turn off autocomplete only on fields that are sensitive in nature. Browsers have tools that let you differentiate form fields:

```
<form method="POST" action="/saveData">
    <input type="text" name="regular" />
    <input type="text" name="sensitive" autocomplete="off" />
    <input type="submit" value="Submit" />
</form>
```

The selective approach lets you protect your customers from leaking their data through the browser while still letting them enjoy the benefits of using autocomplete.

Browsers rely on aggressive caching to speed up page loads, but it becomes a security issue if pages with sensitive information are stored in the cache. Sure, it's nice that the page with your medical records loads fast thanks to the cache, but it also means anyone who can get to the cache can see your records. This is why pages dealing with sensitive data should have caching turned off.

You do this by setting the Cache-Control header to the appropriate value. The most common choice is to set the header to no-cache, because this instructs the browser to re-request the page before showing it to the user. The alternative is to set the header to no-store, which instructs the browser not to write the contents of the response to disk (the cache). From a security standpoint, no-store is the better choice.

You can accomplish this by adding just one line before your reponse-sending function:

```
// Set the header so it is not stored
res.header('Cache-Control', 'no-store');

res.send(data);
```

A better way is to create middleware you can reuse or set before an entire section of the application path that deals with sensitive information:

```
// Define middleware
function noStore(req, res, next) {
    res.header('Cache-Control', 'no-store'); // Set the header so it is not stored
    next(); // Continue
}

// Use middleware
app.get('/data', noStore, function (req, res, next) {
    var data = 'Let this be our sensitive data';

    res.send(data);
});
```

You may be tempted to just set the no-cache header to the entire website, but that would increase server load and affect performance. And that might wind up costing more money than a breach would. Think carefully where you use no-cache.

If your application is collecting sensitive data, you can ramp up the security level by setting up proper XSS protection and being smart about how you use autocomplete and cache. Next, let's see how you can be safe while transporting the data to the server.

## Securely Transfer Data in Your Application

Just collecting the data isn't sufficient. You need to process it before you store it. Let's look at how you can use SSL when transferring the data. You also need to think about what you want to log on the server.

We've already discussed how important it is to use SSL on your website in *Use TLS and SSL to Secure Your Connections*, on page 25. When you're working with sensitive information, securely transporting data using SSL becomes essential. Any page that collects or shows sensitive information to the client must be served over HTTPS; otherwise the traffic can be sniffed and the data exposed. HTTPS needs to be implemented throughout the application since attackers could still hijack the session from insecure traffic and gain access to sensitive data.

In *Decide What Gets Logged*, on page 29, we discussed in length how important it is to properly log requests and errors. Logs let you later trace why certain steps were taken with the website. You can see who performed the action, giving you accountability.

But if you write some or all of the sensitive information handled by the app into the logs because you're trying to generate good and effective logs, you have a problem. This is a common mistake with serious consequences. The risk of sensitive data being exposed is considerable when you consider that logs are rarely encrypted.

Make sure your logs don't contain sensitive information. That doesn't mean you can't log anything related to sensitive information, because that would mean you'd be blind to what's happening with one of the critical parts of the application. Instead, mask the information in the logs. One example is to rewrite the credit card number so that it looks like ****-****-****-1234.

You should now know what you need to securely protect your data as it moves from the browser to the server. Now let's look at how you can secure the data that's being stored.

## Secure the Data Stored Within Your Application

In the previous sections we looked at how to protect the data when the application collects it in the browser and when the application transfers it to the server. These steps focus on short-term protection because the data is present only for a short time. In this section, let's look at how to protect your data for the long term. If you're saving it in storage, you want to keep it for a long time, right? As long as you have the data saved somewhere, someone will try to target it in an attack.

### Don't Hoard Data

The easiest way to protect your application is to not store any sensitive information at all. This is certainly not always possible, but every piece of information that you don't need should be discarded as soon as possible. For example, if you shift the burden of credit card processing to a third-party service, you simplify your security model and speed up development. Of course, you must make sure the third-party software is trustworthy and secure.

Attackers can't steal data that you don't have. Marketing might love data hoarding, but it isn't good security.

Let's look at how to protect your data that's been saved to the file system against overexposure. We'll also cover encryption so that even if all your other defenses fail, the thieves can't do anything with the data.

### Don't Exhibit the Data More Than You Have To

Exposing too much information is a common problem in web applications. It happens because the server is misconfigured or because there's no mechanism to stop path traversal. Anyone can access materials even if they're not authorized.

Oversharing was a common configuration problem in LAMP stacks because Apache had a default directory-sharing configuration that tried to disallow files of a certain type. Fortunately for us, Node.js doesn't thrust a sharing configuration onto developers by default. But it's easy to introduce this error yourself.

Can you spot the problem in the following code?

```
chp-13-sensitive-data/oversharing/app.js
'use strict';

var express = require('express');
var app = express();

app.use(express.static(__dirname));

app.get('/', function(req, res){
    res.send('<script src="/public/main.js"></script>');
});

app.listen(3000);
```

Consider everything we've discussed so far, and you'll see that the issue lies with this line:

```
app.use(express.static(__dirname));
```

The problem is that it gives public file access to the whole application directory, which means that anyone can request files in the directory. Visiting /app.js would show you the application file, for example.

This isn't a big issue for this example because the file itself doesn't reveal any secrets. But mistakes like this can give attackers access to configuration files (with passwords) or code files, where they can look for flaws. It's an easy mistake to make that has serious consequences.

In order to avoid this issue, place public files in a separate folder and share only that folder. I also suggest using a specific path like this:

```
app.use('/public', express.static(__dirname + '/public'));
```

Sometimes you want to use proxies in front of your Node application—like the recommended use of nginx, lighttpd, or H2O for file serving.[1]

---

1. http://nginx.org, http://www.lighttpd.net, and https://h2o.example.net/index.html.

In those configurations you have to make sure that the proxy server itself is properly configured and doesn't allow access to files it's not supposed to.

Oversharing isn't the only thing to worry about. Let's follow up on our static file-serving problems with the path traversal attack. This is an attack vector that tries to break out of the intended public folder and access files that are not supposed to be accessible by using specially crafted strings.

This attack vector used to be so common that servers and libraries like express.static() added their own defenses. If you don't use the libraries, you'll need to roll your own protection. You must understand what's happening before you can set up a robust protection mechanism. Let's take a quick look.

Here's an app that serves files by building the path from query parameters:

chp-13-sensitive-data/traversal/app.js
```
'use strict';

var express = require('express');
var fs = require('fs');
var app = express();

//Construct path
function getPath(filename) {
    return __dirname + '/public/' + filename;
}

app.get('/', function (req, res) {
    if(!req.query.file) {
        res.sendStatus(404);
        return;
    }
    var filePath = getPath(req.query.file);
    var stream = fs.createReadStream(filePath);

    //Handle errors
    stream.on('error', function (err) {
        var status = err.code === 'ENOENT' ? 404 : 500;
        res.sendStatus(status);
    });

    stream.pipe(res);
});

app.listen(3000);
```

You could then ask for a file like /?file=data.json and the server would send you the file. This might look okay, because you're constructing the path with the /public folder inside. However, attackers can use the file system's upward traversal property, ask for /?file=../app.js, and get the contents of app.js. The path-traversal possibilities don't stop there, since you could access *any* file the server process can, including system password files and keys.

Fortunately in Node.js it's easy to set up a robust defense against path traversal. You simply need to construct the absolute path and check that it starts with the absolute path of your expected public folders.

Let's modify the path construction function to add a validation step to check if the path is what you expect it to be:

chp-13-sensitive-data/traversal/app-fixed.js
```
var path = require('path');
var root = path.join(__dirname, '/public');
//Construct absolute path
function getPath(filename) {
    return path.join(root,  filename);
}
//Validate path
function validate(filePath) {
    // Expect the filepath to start with
    // our public root path
    return filePath.indexOf(root) === 0;
}
```

chp-13-sensitive-data/traversal/app-fixed.js
```
var filePath = getPath(req.query.file);
if(!validate(filePath)) {
    res.sendStatus(404);
    return;
}
```

---

**Not Only Read**

A common mistake is expecting path-traversal attacks only when requesting files from the server. *That's far from true.* In fact, it's often useful for attackers to use path-traversal attacks when uploading files to the server, because people tend to forget path traversal in these situations.

Write path traversal allows attackers to overwrite server files and even the /etc/passwd file to gain access to the server, even if the server is running with hightened security privileges. So it's important to be vigilant with path checks when using user input in file path construction.

Limiting public file access to specific controlled folders or files and always constructing and validating absolute paths before actual file access allows you to make sure that you're safe against being overly open with your data.

## Encrypt Your Data so That Attackers Can't Use It

Don't rely on external defenses to protect sensitive and valuable data such as credit card numbers. It takes only a single mistake for an attacker to find a way through your injection defenses and access the database. And then suddenly all your hard work has been lost—because they got everything.

Encryption gives you in-depth protection. Even if your data is stolen, it's not readable without proper keys, providing another important layer of protection.

There are two methods you can follow. The first is to encrypt everything with a master key. It's usually easier to implement, because all data is encrypted and decrypted with the same key. The second is to use a separate key for every user. This ensures that the site administrators don't have access to sensitive information and that attackers have to work harder to get at it. To do this, you have to be able to remove administrators' ability to access encryption keys.

To put it even more simply, trust the administrators, or design the system so that you don't need to trust the administrators.

Let's start by looking at how to implement a master key protection on your database. We'll skip authentication and authorization and start by setting up your routes for handling the form and requests for credit card creation and retrieval:

chp-13-sensitive-data/encrypt/app.js
```
'use strict';

var bodyParser = require('body-parser');
var express = require('express');
var app = express();

var CC = require('./models/cc');

app.get('/cc', function (req, res) {
    var form = '<form method="POST">' +
        '<input autocomplete="off" name="cc" />' +
        '<input type="submit" value="Submit" />' +
        '</form>';
    res.send(form);
});
```

```
app.post('/cc', bodyParser.urlencoded({extended: false}), function (req, res) {
    // Create creditcard from post data
    CC.create(req.body, function (err, cc) {

        //Had an error
        if(err) {
            console.error(err);
            res.sendStatus(500);
            return;
        }

        res.redirect('/cc/' + cc._id);
    });
});

app.get('/cc/:id', function (req, res) {
    // Find creditcard by using id
    CC.findOne({_id: req.params.id}, function (err, cc) {

        // Had an error
        if(err) {
            console.error(err);
            res.sendStatus(500);
            return;
        }
        // Didn't find
        if(!cc) {
            res.sendStatus(404);
            return;
        }

        res.json(cc);
    });
});

app.listen(3000);
```

Next, we'll create your database schema:

chp-13-sensitive-data/encrypt/models/cc-unsecure.js
```
'use strict';

var db = require('../lib/db');

var schema = db.Schema({
    cc: {type: String, required: true}
});

module.exports = db.model('CC', schema);
```

And finally, we'll connect to the database in your db.js:

```
chp-13-sensitive-data/encrypt/lib/db.js
'use strict';

var args = require('minimist')(process.argv);
var mongoose = require('mongoose');

if(!args.d) {
    console.log('This example requires the -d (mongoose db) command line variable');
    process.exit();
}

mongoose.connect(args.d);

module.exports = mongoose;
```

Now you have an application that allows you to store a credit card number in the database and retrieve it based on an identifier. But if someone were to gain access to the database itself, then the attacker could simply request all credit cards and that would be bad. So let's use the built-in crypto module to encrypt and decrypt data.

---

**Cipher Algorithms to Use**

 The following examples implement the aes192 algorithm, but the available algorithms for the crypto module are determined by the underlying OpenSSL installation. On recent releases, openssl list-cipher-algorithms will display the available cipher algorithms.

First, let's create a module to provide the encrypt() and decrypt() methods:

```
chp-13-sensitive-data/encrypt/lib/crypt.js
'use strict';

var args = require('minimist')(process.argv);
var crypto = require('crypto');

if(!args.k) {
    console.log('This example requires the -k (key) command line variable');
    process.exit();
}

var masterKey = args.k;    // Get master key from command line

// A function to perform encryption
function encrypt(data) {
    // Create cipher and encrypt value
    var enc = crypto.createCipher('aes192', masterKey);
    enc.end(data);
    var encrypted = enc.read(); // Read the buffer
```

```
    // We will store the data in base64 format, because utf8 will
    // cause problems - the various characters in utf8 can break or be
    // lost in the storage/retrieval process
    return encrypted.toString('base64');
}

// A function to perform decryption
function decrypt(data) {
    // Create decipher
    var dec = crypto.createDecipher('aes192', masterKey);

    // Create buffer from encrypted value and decrypt
    var encrypted = new Buffer(data, 'base64');
    dec.end(encrypted);

    // Read data and convert back to utf8
    return dec.read().toString('utf8');
}

module.exports.encrypt = encrypt;
module.exports.decrypt = decrypt;
```

And now mongoose lets us use the pre save and pre init hooks to seamlessly encrypt and decrypt data when inserting and retrieving from the database:

chp-13-sensitive-data/encrypt/models/cc.js

```
'use strict';

var db = require('../lib/db');
var crypt = require('../lib/crypt');

var schema = db.Schema({
    cc: {type: String, required: true}
});

// Define a pre save hook to encrypt
schema.pre('save', function (next) {
    // Encrypt the creditcard
    this.cc = crypt.encrypt(this.cc);
    next();
});

// Define a pre init hook to decrypt
schema.pre('init', function (next, data) {
    // Decrypt the credit card
    data.cc = crypt.decrypt(data.cc);
    next();
});

module.exports = db.model('CC', schema);
```

From the outside, the application behaves exactly as it did before. Attackers trying to access the database directly won't see a nice list of credit card numbers but rather something like the following output:

```
{
    "_id" : ObjectId("55a3c200ef5ee77978c1e2cb"),
    "cc" : "+2G/iu05w3Qtk2nai0x6rQ==",
    "__v" : 0
}
```

And without access to the key that was used to encrypt this data, they won't be able to use it. Here lies the weakness of this method—the effectiveness is determined by the security of the key. Don't store the key on the production machine. It's better to just load it into memory.

There should be a gap between the production machine attack vectors and the key storage attack vectors. The security of these machines shouldn't be linked, because you don't want an attacker to be able to access the other machine after breaking into the first one.

For some environments, the fact that the administrators still have access to the database and the master key is a problem. You may not want administrators to be able to decrypt the contents of the database if it contains sensitive information. This is where the second method comes into play—encrypting all values with user-specific keys.

There are several different approaches to encrypting data so that the site administrators are not the gatekeepers. But you cannot store the user's key, since that defeats the purpose of not letting anyone else have access to it.

One method is to give the keys to the users and let them upload the keys to decrypt the data. This isn't very user friendly, but depending on the application's security needs, it might be viable.

Another method—and far simpler—is to do *double encryption*. You store the encryption key on the user model but encrypt it with the user's password. Since the password is hashed, the administrators won't know the password. This prevents them from decrypting the key used to encrypt the data.

Look at the process flow in the following diagram. When the user registers with the application, you generate a key and encrypt the data with that key. You then use the supplied password to encrypt the key.

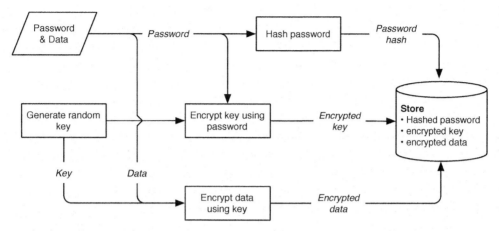

And when the user logs in, you decrypt the key using the password and store it in the session, as shown here.

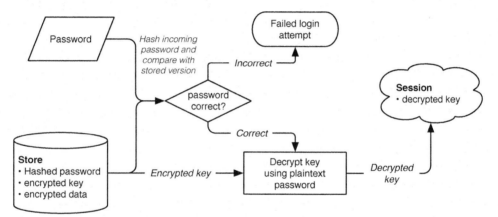

When you need to work with the encrypted data, you can use the key from the session to decrypt it, as in the following diagram.

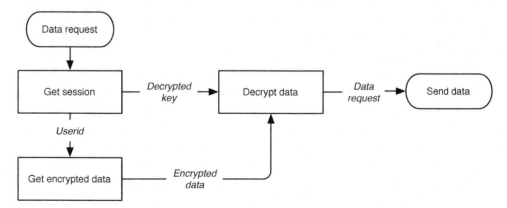

Using this approach, you separate the keys used for the encryption of the sensitive data from the administrators themselves. This way the administrators don't have access to the data, and attackers don't have a single master key to obtain but instead have to break every account separately.

---

**Using Password Instead of Key**

It might seem like less trouble to simply do the encryption with the user's password and skip the intermediate key. Don't do this, because that would mean saving the user passwords in plain text to the session. If the session is compromised in any way, both the encrypted data and the password will be exposed. If you use an intermediate key, the password at least stays safe.

---

By encrypting the sensitive information you select to store in your servers, you'll provide a great deal more security to your customers (unless you distribute the keys liberally). And with that you'll have completed your data protection from the client to the storage itself.

You may be tempted to just encrypt and decrypt all your data exchanges for a high level of security. *Don't.* Cryptography is a resource-heavy process, and doing it for data that's not sensitive is a waste of resources that, depending on the data amount, might cost you a lot of money. Use encryption sparingly and only where needed.

## Wrapping Up

Not all data is created equal, and in this chapter we covered how to protect the most important pieces of data. Your customers would not like their information to fall into the attackers' hands. You learned why you have to protect against XSS attacks, disable caching, use SSL, not log sensitive data, limit how you share server files, and encrypt sensitive pieces of information.

You have data security down. Let's move on to how you can systematically harden your existing code and build applications faster with third-party modules without compromising your overall security.

*The secret of all victory lies in the organization*
*of the non-obvious.*

➤ *Marcus Aurelius*

# CHAPTER 14

# Secure the Existing Codebase

Over the course of this book, we discussed various attack methods and how attackers target the weak points in your application. You learned how to protect your application by strengthening those weak points. When you start writing new code, you should now know how to apply everything we've discussed so far to avoid making common mistakes. It gives you a starting point to prevent users from becoming victims.

But you don't always get to start with a brand-new application. Most of the time, you're working with an existing codebase or using third-party code. By the end of this chapter, you should be able to analyze and secure existing code.

Modern applications are so complex and development deadlines so tight that it's no longer possible to expect developers to write an application from start to finish. Developers tend to work in teams and take advantage of more than 200,000 different packages developed by the vibrant Node.js community. These packages let you drastically speed up development by reusing existing code.

You may now feel confident in your ability to write secure code, but you don't know if the code and modules written by others are also secure. In this chapter, we look at how to analyze existing code to find weaknesses and how the analysis changes when looking at third-party modules. You'll learn to validate the security of the entire application. By the end of this book, you'll know how to secure your application, regardless of whether you wrote it entirely from scratch or some components were written by someone else.

## Perform a Risk Assessment First

I know you're itching to open your code file and get down to business, but you have a few things to take care of first. Before spending your valuable time and energy building a Fort Knox for your application, make sure you need to do that.

Yes, I'm telling you to perform a risk assessment.

A risk assessment determines which security measures you should implement and which you don't have to. From a security perspective, implementing all defenses to the maximum level is always best. In reality, there's a definite financial trade-off. Multiple methodologies are available on how to conduct a risk assessment, but here's a brief overview of what the process entails, as shown in the following diagram.

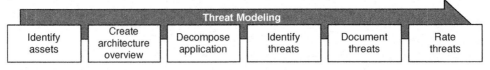

First, identify all the assets that are related to your application (servers, data, and so on). Then analyze your application and write down all the risks to your application that you can think of. This list should include, but not be limited to, situations such as losing client information, website defacement, and site downtime. Then estimate the losses associated with each situation and the costs to recover from each one. Once you have the dollar figures for each risk, estimate the likelihood of each one occurring. Finally, estimate the cost of implementing the mitigation mechanisms for each risk. Use the information derived with this method to determine if the cost of defenses is financially reasonable.

The implementation cost may be exorbitant, but if the losses associated with losing client data are heavy and the odds of a breach are high, then it may make sense to mitigate the issues, no matter how expensive.

Of course, I greatly simplified the process. For a more thorough understanding of how to conduct a risk assessment, refer to the websites for OWASP Risk Rating Methodology[1] and OWASP Threat Risk Modeling.[2]

Now that you know what security levels are appropriate, let's go back to the basics. It's not just about focusing on code quality or making sure you're

---

1.  https://www.owasp.org/index.php/OWASP_Risk_Rating_Methodology
2.  https://www.owasp.org/index.php/Threat_Risk_Modeling

handling malicious inputs and request manipulation attempts correctly. You must remember that the most secure application will still be targeted if it's deployed on a Swiss-cheese-like server. Don't just throw root access to anyone who asks, for example.

Before you proceed with this chapter, take a moment to review Chapter 2, *Set Up the Environment*, on page 11 and Chapter 3, *Start Connecting*, on page 23 and commit the contents to memory. Check how you're deploying your application. Having a solid foundation for your infrastructure is vital for any security-sensitive application.

## Test Your Application's Code Quality

The first thing to get right when starting *a white box analysis* on your application is to validate your own code. I assume we're not talking about one file with fewer than a hundred lines of code. Therefore, meticulously going over every line of code by hand isn't feasible.

An important part of writing a secure web application is maintaining code quality. Security errors frequently start as simple coding mistakes that can be exploited by attackers. Instability can easily be used to launch denial-of-service attacks.

Maintaining code quality as the team and application grow can be daunting, especially by hand. Fortunately, tools such as JSLint[3] and JSHint.[4] are available. They perform static analysis on your JavaScript code and generate error reports on non-optimal programming methods.

These tools also check for security-related issues, such as making sure you're running all functions in strict mode and that you're using strict comparison operators instead of == and !=. They also disallow changes to native prototypes and make sure variables are not being used before they're defined.

Another common example is looping over object properties without using hasOwnProperty(). There are many other issues, but the idea is to make the code cleaner and uniformly understandable to reduce the number of potential bugs and logic errors.

While there are various ways to run static analysis on your code, the recommended approach is to integrate the tests into your build or publish process. Don't treat it as a one-off test and call it done. JSLint and JSHint both have packages for all major build managers like Grunt and Gulp, or you can create

---

3. http://www.jslint.com
4. http://jshint.com

your own build script. Ideally, you should run the static analysis every time you're about to publish or commit your changes. Many version control systems provide precommit hooks so that you can run some sort of static analysis every time you make changes to the code.

npm has a prepublish script that can be configured to run a command every time you publish your package. It looks something like this:

```
{
  "name": "ethopia-waza",
  "description": "a delightfully fruity code",
  "version": "1.2.3",
  "devDependencies": {
    "jshint": "*"
  },
  "scripts": {
    "prepublish": "./node_modules/jshint/bin/jshint ./*/**.js"
  },
  "main": "lib/waza.js"
}
```

## Analyze Your Application's Data Flow

At this point in the process, you know your code doesn't have major quality issues that could cause breakages. Let's move on to deeper analysis.

The most effective way to secure your application is to first understand it. You must grasp how your application does what it does, and to do that you must follow the data.

*Input/output* (I/O) operations are the core of any web application and are something Node.js excels at. But what's actually going on? See the following graphic.

You need to understand why your application behaves in a certain way and how it handles your requests. That's the only way you'll know all the possible permutations of what the application can do, and you can limit the list accordingly. An in-depth understanding of the application also helps you narrow your search area when hunting for vulnerabilities.

To start, you can narrow your search field by grouping request handling into various categories: static requests, insecure and secure data requests, content-modifying requests, and client-side variables, as shown in this diagram.

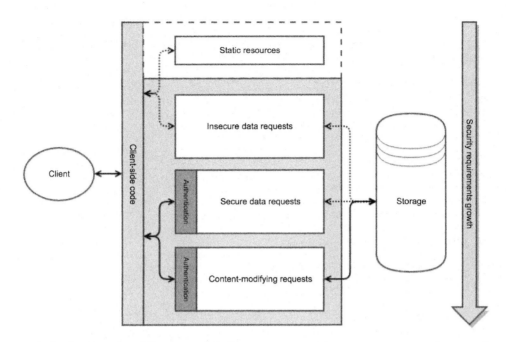

Let's look at each of them in detail.

## Identify Static Requests in Your Code

Static requests have no user input besides the URL path. This includes static files and paths that serve generic content, such as the home page and login page. While the pages served can be dynamic, such as showing the latest five stories, they shouldn't rely on user input to generate the contents displayed. These requests don't have session data, so they're public by definition.

A path generating dynamic content like this is static:

```
chp-14-secure/data-flow.js
function getRandomNumbers() {
    var randoms = [];
    for(var i = 0; i < 5; i++) {
        randoms.push(Math.random());
    }
    return randoms;
}

app.get('/', function (req, res) {
    res.json(getRandomNumbers());
});
```

A path serving static content like this is not because it checks for the user's logged-in status based on the session, which is based on a cookie, a type of user input:

```
chp-14-secure/data-flow.js
var session = require('express-session');
var cookieParser = require('cookie-parser');
var easySession = require('easy-session');

app.use(cookieParser());
app.use(session({
    secret: 'this is a nice secret',
    resave: false,
    saveUninitialized: true
}));
app.use(easySession.main(session));

app.get('/login', function (req, res) {
    if(req.session.isLoggedIn()) {
        res.redirect('/');
        return;
    }
    res.send('<form></form>');
});
```

You don't want the user to be able to force the server into using the input in any way. Static resource serving is commonly targeted with path traversal attacks. This is why you need to be concerned with those paths and secure them as needed.

### Identify Insecure and Secure Data Requests in Your Application

Insecure data requests are requests for dynamic content that don't need authorization. These requests use GET and HEAD requests as well as path, query, and cookie parameters to determine what content to serve on the page. Since the pages serve only public content, the user doesn't have to worry about authentication.

The following example shows a data request that's insecure because it uses the user-provided value to display data. The problem is, as written, it lets an unauthorized user provide that information:

```
chp-14-secure/data-flow-insecure.js
app.get('/:path', function (req, res) {
    res.sendFile(req.params.path + '.html');
});
```

You can use session variables as long as you aren't relying on the user's identity. Let's look at two versions of the same code, one secure and the other not:

chp-14-secure/data-flow-insecure.js

```javascript
// This is an insecure request
app.get('/session', function (req, res) {
    if(!req.session.nr || typeof req.session.nr !== 'number') {
        req.session.nr = 0;
    }
    req.session.nr++;
    res.send('Request nr: ' + req.session.nr);
});


// This is not an insecure request
app.use(easySession.main(session));
app.get('/login', function (req, res) {
    if(req.session.isLoggedIn()) {
        res.redirect('/');
        return;
    }
    res.send('<form></form>');
});
```

Once you've identified insecure data requests in your application, the best thing to do is to whitelist all user input wherever possible. This is the single most effective protective measure you can take with these paths:

chp-14-secure/data-flow-insecure.js

```javascript
var allowedFiles = [
    'index',
    'login',
    'static'
];
app.get('/:path', function (req, res) {
    // Validate that it is an expected path
    if(allowedFiles.indexOf(req.params.path) === -1) {
        res.send(404);
        return;
    }
    res.sendFile(req.params.path + '.html');
});
```

In fact, you should go through the handler's call stack and make sure every function relying on user input or a value based on user input has embedded whitelist checks. You'll have to use other sanitizing methods if whitelisting isn't an option, but you still want to limit all possible inputs.

Perform sanity checks on all variables that are part of the request, including the ones you introduce via cookies as well as those created by client-side code. When introducing sanitizing methods, take into account the locations and functions using the variables, such as the database, the file system, and the command line, because you'll have to use the methods differently depending on location.

Don't forget about second-hand validation; you need to validate data previously inserted into storage by users and then retrieved. Let's look at web comments, since they're one of the most common examples of second-hand input. Users post comments from the application, and the server saves the data in storage. When the page is displayed later, the application may look at the timestamp to retrieve and display some of the comments. These comments need to be validated.

You also need to look at secure data requests. These are similar to the insecure requests, except they're used to serve restricted data. The output depends on the user's identity. You perform the same checks on secure data requests as you do on insecure data requests. Make sure the user's identity and access level match what is being requested. This is a good time to review access checks as discussed in Chapter 9, *Set Up Access Control*, on page 111.

## Identify Content-Modifying Requests in Your Application

The next group is the one most prone to errors and requires thorough checking. These requests modify or store information in your application and change the application's state. We're talking about PUT, POST, PATCH, and DELETE requests. We've discussed some of the key factors already: checking access rights for secure requests, limiting input data, validating input data based on location, and being vigilant for errors. What you also need to do is to check for the request's origin to prevent CSRF. You can review how to prevent CSRF attacks in Chapter 12, *Avoid Request Forgery*, on page 161.

When accepting input from the client, be as strict as possible. This means that when you expect a path to process POST requests you do not accept GET or any other type besides POST. The same goes for input variables—do not use generic parameter access methods like req.param() that take input from the path, body, or query depending on where it's found first. For example, if you expect a POST with a body, then don't accept query or path parameters as substitutes. Doing so would create confusion and in some cases allow attackers to exploit the order in which validation and usage are performed.

Users can always add unexpected parameters to requests. Remove these before running the rest of the code.

Nothing in the following code prevents the attacker from adding the role parameter to the request being submitted. Even though the role isn't one of the values included in the form, it doesn't matter because the attacker can create administrator users with the parameter:

chp-14-secure/data-flow-clean.js
```
// Define user model
var userSchema = new mongoose.Schema({
    username:  { type: String, required: true, index: { unique: true } },
    password: { type: String, required: true}, // this should be hashed
    role: {
        type: String,
        enum: ['guest', 'user', 'admin'],
        required: true,
        default: 'user'
    }
});

var User = mongoose.model('User', userSchema);

app.post('/user', function (req, res) {
    User.create(req.body, function (err, user) {
        if(err) {
            console.log(err);
            res.send(500);
            return;
        }
        res.send(200);
    });
});
```

In order to prevent these kinds of data modifications, you should clean the input to allow only specified variables. After you remove the extra variables, you should still sanitize what's left:

chp-14-secure/data-flow-clean-correct.js
```
var allowed = [
    'username',
    'password'
];
app.post('/user', function (req, res) {
    var data = {};

    //Filter the input
    allowed.forEach(function (key) {
        data[key] = req.body[key];
    });
```

```
User.create(data, function (err, user) {
    if(err) {
        console.log(err);
        res.send(500);
        return;
    }
    res.send(200);
});
});
```

### Identify and Clean Client-Side Variables Used by Your Application

In the last step, we look at identifying all the variables that affect how client-side code is constructed and clean them to prevent XSS attacks. If your application is just an API, you don't need to worry about this last category. Otherwise, XSS is a major attack vector and must be mitigated. Now is a good time to go over the template and client-side JavaScript files while keeping the lessons from Chapter 11, *Fight Cross-Site Scripts*, on page 139 in mind.

It will be a long and tedious process, but the result should be a secure client for your web app. Employing these methods will make server-side code easier to understand, straightforward to maintain, and harder to attack. So far, we've focused on securing your existing codebase. Let's look at the techniques you'll need for securing third-party code, the modules and libraries written and maintained by someone else.

## If Nothing Else, Use a Helmet

In the previous sections we looked at deeply analyzing your application code to identify various possible attack vectors and setting up mitigation methods for them. While it is the recommended and definitely more effective way to secure your application, it is also usually a lot of work and can take a long time (depending on the size of your codebase). If you find yourself with a gun to your head and only have a minute to set up some defense, then use helmet.

helmet is an express middleware designed to implement HTTP header-based defense for various attack methods we have covered in this book. It is a collection of various other middleware, each designed for a specific attack vector. The use of helmet is simple:

```
var express = require('express');
var app = express();

var helmet = require('helmet');
app.use(helmet()); // Use helmet with default settings
```

Just with those two lines you:

- remove the X-Powered-By header to aggravate enumeration
- set up HSTS headers for HTTP Strict Transport Security
- set X-Download-Options for IE8+ to prevent execution of downloads
- set X-Content-Type-Options: nosniff to prevent MIME Confusion attacks
- set the X-Frame-Options header to prevent clickjacking
- set the X-XSS-Protection header to help mitigate XSS

You should add helmet.csp as discussed in *Prevent XSS Through Configuration*, on page 142.

```
var express = require('express');
var app = express();

var helmet = require('helmet');
app.use(helmet());              // Use helmet with default settings
app.use(helmet.csp({           // Use CSP with minimal settings
  defaultSrc: ["'self'"]
}));
```

So with three lines, you set up decent protection against various attack methods—a quick and easy win upon which you can expand your stronger defense once you dodge the bullet deadline.

## Clean the Modules You Use in Your Code

Instead of developing applications from scratch, we typically integrate existing code and libraries. This is especially common for Node.js applications, since NPM has over 200,000 published packages (and growing!). The fact that there's a vast library of existing code that can be plugged into any project is one of the things that makes Node.js development fast. However, there's a security trade-off to the speed and convenience.

The packages in the repository vary greatly in code quality, available documentation, maintenance schedule, and even the language (JavaScript, Coffee-Script, C, C++) used. They are developed and maintained by different teams and individuals, making it difficult to have a consistent update cycle.

The list that follows on page 198 shows the modules tree for a typical Node.js project using Express for the framework, Redis for session storage, and Mongoose for MongoDB ORM.

The dependency graph lists a total of fifty-nine different modules installed. From a security standpoint, the fact that there's no vetting process when adding new packages to NPM is concerning. Many of these packages could

```
express@4.13.1                              « (continued from previous column)
├── merge-descriptors@1.0.0
├── array-flatten@1.1.0                     ├── type-is@1.6.5
├── escape-html@1.0.2                       ├───────media-typer@0.3.0
├── cookie@0.1.3                            ├───────mime-types@2.1.3
├── cookie-signature@1.0.6                  ├── send@0.13.0
├── methods@1.1.1                           ├───────destroy@1.0.3
├── fresh@0.3.0                             ├───────statuses@1.2.1
├── range-parser@1.0.2                      ├──────ms@0.7.1
├── vary@1.0.1                              ├──────mime@1.3.4
├── utils-merge@1.0.0                       └───────http-errors@1.3.1
├── etag@1.7.0
├── path-to-regexp@0.1.6               mongoose@4.1.0
├── content-type@1.0.1                      ├── regexp-clone@0.0.1
├── parseurl@1.3.0                          ├── sliced@0.0.5
├── content-disposition@0.5.0              ├── muri@1.0.0
├── serve-static@1.10.0                    ├── mpromise@0.5.4
├── depd@1.0.1                              ├── hooks-fixed@1.1.0
├── qs@4.0.0                                ├── kareem@1.0.1
├── on-finished@2.3.0                      ├── mpath@0.1.1
├──────ee-first@1.1.1                       ├── async@0.9.0
├── finalhandler@0.4.0                     ├── ms@0.1.0
├──────unpipe@1.0.0                         ├── mquery@1.6.1
├── debug@2.2.0                             ├──────debug@2.2.0
├──────ms@0.7.1                             ├──────bluebird@2.9.26
├── proxy-addr@1.0.8                       ├── mongodb@2.0.34
├──────forwarded@0.1.0                      ├───────readable-stream@1.0.31
├──────ipaddr.js@1.0.1                      ├───────mongodb-core@1.2.0
├── accepts@1.2.11                         ├── bson@0.3.2
├──────negotiator@0.5.3                     └───────bson-ext@0.1.10
├──────mime-types@2.1.3
                                       redis@0.12.1
```

contain—either accidentally or maliciously—security vulnerabilities. When developing a security-sensitive application, you have to check all modules and submodules being used.

This can get cumbersome as the number of modules increases, and there's no way around it. Fortunately, community projects are available to help, such as the Node Security Project,[5] which aims to audit all NPM modules and provide Node.js-specific security advice. The project offers a public API to query the database of modules, and a command-line tool nsp that checks the security status of a known package. The use of this tool is simple.

Install it with NPM:

```
npm install nsp -g
```

---

5.   https://nodesecurity.io

And then in your project folder run the check:

```
nsp check
```

This checks your package.json and/or shrinkwrap.json files for packages with known vulnerabilities. If a vulnerable package is found, the output looks like the figure:

```
(+) 1 vulnerabilities found
|           | Regular Expression Denial of Service            |
| Name      | ms                                              |
| Installed | 0.6.2                                           |
| Vulnerable| <=0.7.0                                          |
| Patched   | >0.7.0                                           |
| Path      | connect-redis > debug > ms                      |
| More Info | https://nodesecurity.io/advisories/46           |
```

This gives you a nice overview of what you need to update and why.

Next, let's look at a few things to keep in mind when selecting and working with third-party packages.

## Rules for Choosing Which Package to Use

A great variety of modules are available, and it's difficult to know which ones are safe to use from a security standpoint. While there's no clear-cut way to choose third-party libraries and node modules, we can look at three potential approaches: choosing popular packages, obscuring modules, and writing your own code.

The first choice, popularity, means you choose packages based on how many people are using it or know about it. Look at the community behind the module: is it being maintained by a company committed to that project or used by a large enough group of people? A dedicated company is likely to care about maintaining the package and its reputation. A large userbase means most of the obvious security vulnerabilities have probably been found, reported, and fixed accordingly. These packages are unlikely to contain malicious backdoors.

The size of the userbase should be treated as a soft validation of the package's security, not a guarantee. Since the packages are widely used, they're also more likely to be targeted by attackers looking for vulnerabilities. Bugs can also slip through, as happened with the Heartbleed flaw in OpenSSL. Security flaws in these modules can be used against a lot of targets at once, which is known as a *shotgun attack*.

The other approach is to use packages that aren't so popular or open source to limit exposure. This reduces the possibility of shotgun attacks where the attackers focus on all the users of a particular library. But small, unknown libraries tend to have lower code quality, reduced support, and a less-mature codebase. However, if your application is niche enough, the modules you're interested in may already be specialized and not one of the popular ones in the first place.

Of course, you always have the option to write all your code yourself and disregard all third-party libraries. You have custom code and a complete overview of everything happening within your application. But it is hell on the team, lengthens development time, and is typically not financially or logistically feasible. Even with the knowledge you've gained through this book, you have to accept that you can still make mistakes in your code. With third-party libraries, it's possible that the other developer avoided making that mistake, or it has been found and reported by other users already.

Regardless of which method you follow to choose your packages, you can't just assume they're secure. Trust but verify, remember?

## Audit the Chosen Ones, aka Third-Party Packages

After selecting your modules, invest some time in auditing them. You want to make sure the packages meet a baseline standard for security necessary for your application. There aren't specific rules for audits because each module can vary greatly in code quality and functionality, but I recommend looking at the functionality you're using and the data flow.

First of all, look over the module and check to see which exposed functionality you use and which you don't use. If you don't use a lot of the functionality in the module, then you might be using the wrong package for the job to begin with. Bloated modules tend to complicate your code and create unnecessary dependencies. Try to avoid them.

Then, look over the code to determine what the module does with your input and how the data moves internally within the module. See if any of your input is insecure and vulnerable or somehow maliciously manipulated within the application. This way, you have a clear overview of exactly what the module does with your data.

If the module handles user input before it reaches you, then it must meet the corresponding standards. Don't use eval or similar. Functions shouldn't be invoked without validation. Proper limits have to be defined. If you handle the data before sending it to the module, then you can—and should—perform the validations yourself, unless you're sure the module takes care of it.

The audit helps you look for accidental vulnerabilities, whether they're in your own code or in third-party libraries. But not all vulnerabilities are accidental, and you need to look for the malicious ones, too. Malicious bugs are most likely trying to set a backdoor into your application or gather data. Look for the following: access to the file system and network traffic, code that runs on timeouts, and the package.json scripts.

A module would use corresponding Node.js built-in modules or C/C++ add-ons to access the file system or to relay or set up network traffic. Look for modules using fs, net, http, tls, child_process, cluster, udp, and vm because they're native modules designed to access the file system, relay or set up network traffic, and execute system commands. Beware of custom C/C++ modules that also do this.

If the package has malicious code—other than code written to manipulate user data—it will most likely run when the module is first initialized or after a certain time period has passed. Look for lines of code executed at regular intervals or during startup. Those scripts typically have a descriptors in the package.json.

And I shouldn't have to say this, but avoid installing modules under the root account. You should never give scripts, especially third-party ones, root-access-level rights. If you're installing a package that uses the -g flag for global access, be wary of what you're installing and which account level the script will have.

If you followed the steps outlined here, you should have already caught most of the issues. The audit process is necessary for the whole dependency tree. Now, let's look at how to make sure the modules remain secure over the lifetime of your application.

## Keeping Your Modules Up to Date and Secure

Once you've selected and validated all the modules that you use, you should be good, right? Wrong. You now have to keep an eye out for security fixes for these modules and install them accordingly.

Patches for vulnerabilities, overall improvements, and bug fixes are released for various packages daily. When setting up a secure project that uses third-party NPM modules, you must periodically check for updates on the whole tree. That way, you'll know if any important vulnerabilities or bugs have been fixed and will require an update. At the same time, you must also be careful that updating your modules doesn't introduce any breaking changes in the dependencies. Make sure updates for every module are thoroughly tested on a test server before updating the modules installed on the live server.

We've focused on testing the modules. Let's now have a look at the application as a whole to make sure it's secure.

## Test Your Application Security Thoroughly

Now that you've thoroughly analyzed and secured the application and all its dependencies, it's time to give your application an end-to-end test to see if you've accounted for all well-known attack vectors.

For this you should start by looking up a security checklist provided by web security organizations like OWASP. I personally find the OWASP ASVS (Application Security Verification Standard)[6] to be an excellent guide to checking an application's security implementations. Take the security checklist in hand and go over each bullet point relevant for your application. Have you implemented each of the required measures?

The checklist will help you verify that you've addressed specific pain points. You want your authentication controls to fail securely to prevent attackers from logging in. You want to verify that password entry fields allow passphrases and provide users with minimum strength requirements. Passwords should not have an arbitrary length or complexity limit, for example. Remember to verify account identity authentication functions, such as registration, account recovery, and help. The last thing you want is for the attacker to use a recovery mechanism to get access to the account.

Going over this checklist will give you adequate reassurance only if you have a good understanding of your requirements. I highly recommend performing—or better yet, commissioning—a penetration test on your application. You can hire specialists, or you can do it yourself. Penetration tests help you understand how well the security you implemented works. You should be performing a penetration test on a regular basis to determine your application's overall security.

---

6. https://www.owasp.org/images/5/58/OWASP_ASVS_Version_2.pdf

Thinking like an attacker makes you better at figuring out what needs to be protected. Penetration tests help you develop that skill, and you can get started with the OWASP NodeGoat Project,[7] a vulnerable Node.js web application packed with OWASP Top 10 vulnerabilities. There are plenty of other resources, ranging from lightweight cheat sheets[8] to books like *Hacking: The Art of Exploitation*, by Jon Erickson.[9]

Once you get into performing penetration testing there are loads of tools you can use that do a lot of heavy lifting for you. If you are serious, then I recommend at minimum looking into:

- Metasploit:[10] Popular penetration testing software
- Kali Linux:[11] A Linux build specifically for penetration testing
- Burp suite:[12] A toolkit for testing web applications

## Wrapping Up

In this chapter you learned how to systematically apply your previously acquired knowledge on your existing projects. You learned how to analyze your application to find potential attack points. We also discussed how to audit third-party modules so that you can benefit from the community's existing body of work without compromising your security. Finally, we covered the benefits of performing penetration tests on your code.

This knowledge should help you secure your old projects and start off securely from day one with new projects without feeling overwhelmed or lost.

## Where to Go from Here

Congratulations! You've reached the end of this book. You've learned a lot about defending your applications from attackers and their dark arts. We covered a lot of ground from the basics of JavaScript and server security, all the way to database essentials and client-side security. Is your head swimming with new security concepts?

I don't want to discourage you, but this book just scratched the surface of application security. Exploiting applications for financial or personal gain is

---

7.   https://github.com/OWASP/NodeGoat

8.   https://www.owasp.org/index.php/Web_Application_Security_Testing_Cheat_Sheet

9.   http://www.amazon.com/Hacking-The-Art-Exploitation-Edition/dp/1593271441

10.  http://www.metasploit.com/

11.  https://www.kali.org/

12.  https://portswigger.net/burp/

a big business. New attacks and defense methods are published all the time, and keeping up with them is a big challenge.

There's no such thing as perfect security since any system can be compromised given enough time and effort. Your job, then, is to keep learning about new security attacks, mitigations, and defenses so that you can stay ahead of the curve. Don't forget, attackers will generally go for the low-hanging fruit first. If you don't have any in your code, you buy yourself some time.

Keep reading and learning because there's plenty of material left to cover. We took only a brief glimpse at network and operating system–level security and penetration testing. There are other methods for analyzing systems, prioritizing defenses, and creating appropriate security policies. You need to educate your employees about social engineering attacks. The road ahead is long and full of information, and while it may seem daunting, I invite you to keep educating yourself.

Don't feel overwhelmed by the amount still left to learn. Finishing this book puts you ahead of many developers in terms of being aware about security. Yes, you know a lot, but make sure you apply the knowledge to your Node.js web applications. Until you start practicing secure methods and implement the guidelines in the book, you won't have a secure application. Get out there and apply what you've learned, play with different tools, and keep learning at every opportunity. Remember the words of Benjamin Franklin: "An investment in knowledge pays the best interest."

You've taken your first steps toward securing your Node.js web application. Great job! Keep it up!

# Bibliography

[Cro08]   Douglas Crockford. *JavaScript: The Good Parts*. O'Reilly & Associates, Inc., Sebastopol, CA, 2008.

[Eri08]   Jon Erickson. *Hacking: The Art of Exploitation*. No Starch Press, San Francisco, CA, 2nd, 2008.

[Res09]   John Resig. *Secrets of the JavaScript Ninja*. Manning Publications Co., Greenwich, CT, 2009.

# Index

# The Modern Web

Get up to speed on the latest JavaScript techniques.


## Deliver Audacious Web Apps with Ember 2

It's time for web development to be fun again, time to
write engaging and attractive apps – fast – in this brisk
tutorial. Build a complete user interface in a few lines
of code, create reusable web components, access
RESTful services and cache the results for performance, and use JavaScript modules to bring abstraction to your code. Find out how you can get your crucial app infrastructure up and running quickly, so you
can spend your time on the stuff great apps are made
of: features.

Matthew White
(154 pages) ISBN: 9781680500783. $24
*https://pragprog.com/book/mwjsember*


## Reactive Programming with RxJS

Reactive programming is revolutionary. It makes
asynchronous programming clean, intuitive, and robust. Use the RxJS library to write complex programs
in a simple way, unifying asynchronous mechanisms
such as callbacks and promises into a powerful data
type: the Observable. Learn to think about your programs as streams of data that you can transform by
expressing *what* should happen, instead of having to
painstakingly program *how* it should happen. Manage
real-world concurrency and write complex flows of
events in your applications with ease.

Sergi Mansilla
(142 pages) ISBN: 9781680501292. $18
*https://pragprog.com/book/smreactjs*

# Put the "Fun" in Functional

Elixir puts the "fun" back into functional programming, on top of the robust, battle-tested, industrial-strength environment of Erlang. Add in the unparalleled beauty and ease of the Phoenix web framework, and enjoy the web again!

## Programming Elixir

You want to explore functional programming, but are put off by the academic feel (tell me about monads just one more time). You know you need concurrent applications, but also know these are almost impossible to get right. Meet Elixir, a functional, concurrent language built on the rock-solid Erlang VM. Elixir's pragmatic syntax and built-in support for metaprogramming will make you productive and keep you interested for the long haul. This book is *the* introduction to Elixir for experienced programmers.

Maybe you need something that's closer to Ruby, but with a battle-proven environment that's unrivaled for massive scalability, concurrency, distribution, and fault tolerance. Maybe the time is right for the Next Big Thing. Maybe it's *Elixir*.

Dave Thomas
(340 pages) ISBN: 9781937785581. $36
*https://pragprog.com/book/elixir*

## Programming Phoenix

Don't accept the compromise between fast and beautiful: you can have it all. Phoenix creator Chris McCord, Elixir creator José Valim, and award-winning author Bruce Tate walk you through building an application that's fast and reliable. At every step, you'll learn from the Phoenix creators not just what to do, but why. Packed with insider insights, this definitive guide will be your constant companion in your journey from Phoenix novice to expert, as you build the next generation of web applications.

Chris McCord, Bruce Tate, and José Valim
(230 pages) ISBN: 9781680501452. $34
*https://pragprog.com/book/phoenix*

# Long Live the Command Line!

Use tmux and Vim for incredible mouse-free productivity.

## tmux

Your mouse is slowing you down. The time you spend context switching between your editor and your consoles eats away at your productivity. Take control of your environment with tmux, a terminal multiplexer that you can tailor to your workflow. Learn how to customize, script, and leverage tmux's unique abilities and keep your fingers on your keyboard's home row.

Brian P. Hogan
(88 pages) ISBN: 9781934356968. $16.25
*https://pragprog.com/book/bhtmux*

## Practical Vim, Second Edition

Vim is a fast and efficient text editor that will make you a faster and more efficient developer. It's available on almost every OS, and if you master the techniques in this book, you'll never need another text editor. In more than 120 Vim tips, you'll quickly learn the editor's core functionality and tackle your trickiest editing and writing tasks. This beloved bestseller has been revised and updated to Vim 7.4 and includes three brand-new tips and five fully revised tips.

Drew Neil
(354 pages) ISBN: 9781680501278. $29
*https://pragprog.com/book/dnvim2*

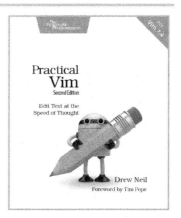

# The Pragmatic Bookshelf

The Pragmatic Bookshelf features books written by developers for developers. The titles continue the well-known Pragmatic Programmer style and continue to garner awards and rave reviews. As development gets more and more difficult, the Pragmatic Programmers will be there with more titles and products to help you stay on top of your game.

# Visit Us Online

### This Book's Home Page
*https://pragprog.com/book/kdnodesec*
Source code from this book, errata, and other resources. Come give us feedback, too!

### Register for Updates
*https://pragprog.com/updates*
Be notified when updates and new books become available.

### Join the Community
*https://pragprog.com/community*
Read our weblogs, join our online discussions, participate in our mailing list, interact with our wiki, and benefit from the experience of other Pragmatic Programmers.

### New and Noteworthy
*https://pragprog.com/news*
Check out the latest pragmatic developments, new titles and other offerings.

# Save on the eBook

Save on the eBook versions of this title. Owning the paper version of this book entitles you to purchase the electronic versions at a terrific discount.

PDFs are great for carrying around on your laptop—they are hyperlinked, have color, and are fully searchable. Most titles are also available for the iPhone and iPod touch, Amazon Kindle, and other popular e-book readers.

Buy now at *https://pragprog.com/coupon*

# Contact Us

| | |
|---|---|
| Online Orders: | *https://pragprog.com/catalog* |
| Customer Service: | *support@pragprog.com* |
| International Rights: | *translations@pragprog.com* |
| Academic Use: | *academic@pragprog.com* |
| Write for Us: | *http://write-for-us.pragprog.com* |
| Or Call: | +1 800-699-7764 |